IN THE MORNING GLOW; SHORT STORIES

Published @ 2017 Trieste Publishing Pty Ltd

ISBN 9780649613892

In the Morning Glow; Short Stories by Roy Rolfe Gilson

Except for use in any review, the reproduction or utilisation of this work in whole or in part in any form by any electronic, mechanical or other means, now known or hereafter invented, including xerography, photocopying and recording, or in any information storage or retrieval system, is forbidden without the permission of the publisher, Trieste Publishing Pty Ltd, PO Box 1576 Collingwood, Victoria 3066 Australia.

All rights reserved.

Edited by Trieste Publishing Pty Ltd.
Cover @ 2017

This book is sold subject to the condition that it shall not, by way of trade or otherwise, be lent, re-sold, hired out, or otherwise circulated without the publisher's prior consent in any form or binding or cover other than that in which it is published and without a similar condition including this condition being imposed on the subsequent purchaser.

www.triestepublishing.com

ROY ROLFE GILSON

IN THE MORNING GLOW; SHORT STORIES

[See page 187

"'WHAT A BEAUTIFUL DREAM!'"

IN THE MORNING GLOW

Short Stories

by

ROY ROLFE GILSON

AUTHOR OF "WHEN LOVE IS YOUNG"

ILLUSTRATED

NEW YORK AND LONDON
HARPER & BROTHERS
PUBLISHERS 1902

TO

MY WIFE

Contents

	PAGE
GRANDFATHER	3
GRANDMOTHER	33
WHILE AUNT JANE PLAYED	51
LITTLE SISTER	61
OUR YARD	85
THE TOY GRENADIER	107
FATHER	127
MOTHER	165

Illustrations

"'WHAT A BEAUTIFUL DREAM!'"	*Frontispiece*	
"WHEN GRANDFATHER WORE HIS WHITE VEST YOU WALKED LIKE OTHER FOLKS"	*Facing p.*	4
"YOU STOLE SOFTLY TO HIS SIDE"	"	8
"WATCHED HIM MAKE THE BLUE FRAGMENTS INTO THE BLUE PITCHER AGAIN"	"	20
"THE SAIL-BOATS HE WHITTLED FOR YOU ON RAINY DAYS"	"	24
"YOU CLUNG TO HER APRON FOR SUPPORT IN YOUR MUTE AGONY"	"	36
"YOU WATCHED THEM AS THEY WENT DOWN THE WALK TOGETHER"	"	42
"TO AND FRO GRANDMOTHER ROCKED YOU"	"	46
"YOU SAID 'NOW I LAY ME' IN UNISON"	"	62

Illustrations

"MOTHER TUCKED YOU BOTH INTO BED AND KISSED YOU"	Facing p.	68
"THEY TOOK YOU AS FAR AS THE BEDROOM DOOR TO SEE HER"	"	78
"'BAD DREAM, WAS IT, LITTLE CHAP?'"	"	136
"'FATHER, WHAT DO YOU THINK WHEN YOU DON'T SAY ANYTHING, BUT JUST LOOK?'"	"	150
"'MOTHER,' YOU SAID, SOFTLY"	"	162
"THE PICTURE-BOOK"	"	166
"BEFORE YOU WENT TO BED"	"	168

Grandfather

Grandfather

WHEN you gave Grandfather both your hands and put one foot against his knee and the other against his vest, you could walk right up to his white beard like a fly — but you had to hold tight. Sometimes your foot slipped on the knee, but the vest was wider and not so hard, so that when you were that far you were safe. And when you had both feet in the soft middle of the vest, and your body was stiff, and your face was looking right up at the ceiling, Grandfather groaned down deep inside, and that was the sign

In the Morning Glow

that your walk was ended. Then Grandfather crumpled you up in his arms. But on Sunday, when Grandfather wore his white vest, you walked like other folks.

In the morning Grandfather sat in the sun by the wall — the stone wall at the back of the garden, where the golden-rod grew. Grandfather read the paper and smoked. When it was afternoon and Mother was taking her nap, Grandfather was around the corner of the house, on the porch, in the sun—always in the sun, for the sun followed Grandfather wherever he went, till he passed into the house at supper-time. Then the sun went down and it was night.

Grandfather walked with a cane; but even then, with all the three legs he boasted of, you could run the meadow to the big rock before Grandfather had gone halfway. Grandfather's pipe was corn-cob,

"WHEN GRANDFATHER WORE HIS WHITE VEST YOU WALKED LIKE OTHER FOLKS"

Grandfather

and every week he had a new one, for the little brown juice that cuddled down in the bottom of the bowl, and wouldn't come out without a straw, wasn't good for folks, Grandfather said. Old Man Stubbs, who came across the road to see Grandfather, chewed his tobacco, yet the little brown juice did not hurt him at all, he said. Still it was not pleasant to kiss Old Man Stubbs, and Mother said that chewing tobacco was a filthy habit, and that only very old men ever did it nowadays, because lots of people used to do it when Grandfather and Old Man Stubbs were little boys. Probably, you thought, people did not kiss other folks so often then.

One morning Grandfather was reading by the wall, in the sun. You were on the ground, flat, peeping under the grass, and you were so still that a cricket came and teetered on a grass-stalk near at hand.

In the Morning Glow

Two red ants climbed your hat as it lay beside you, and a white worm swung itself from one grass-blade to another, like a monkey. The ground under the apple-trees was broken out with sun-spots. Bees were humming in the red clover. Butterflies lazily flapped their wings and sailed like little boats in a sea of golden-rod and Queen Anne's lace.

"Dee, dee-dee, dee-dee," you sang, and Mr. Cricket sneaked under a plantain leaf. You tracked him to his lair with your finger, and he scuttled away.

"Grandfather."

No reply.

"*Grand*father."

Not a word. Then you looked. Grandfather's paper had slipped to the ground, and his glasses to his lap. He was fast asleep in the sunshine with his head upon his breast. You stole softly to his side

Grandfather

With a long grass you tickled his ear. With a jump he awoke, and you tumbled, laughing, on the grass.

"Ain't you 'shamed?" cried Lizzie-in-the-kitchen, who was hanging out the clothes.

"Huh! Grandfather don't care."

Grandfather never cared. That is one of the things which made him Grandfather. If he had scolded he might have been Father, or even Uncle Ned—but he would not have been Grandfather. So when you spoiled his nap he only said, "H'm," deep in his beard, put on his glasses, and read his paper again.

When it was afternoon, and the sun followed Grandfather to the porch, and you were tired of playing House, or Hop-Toad, or Indian, or the Three Bears, it was only a step from Grandfather's foot to Grandfather's lap. When you sat back

In the Morning Glow

and curled your legs, your head lay in the hollow of Grandfather's shoulder, in the shadow of his white beard. Then Grandfather would say,

"Once upon a time there was a bear . . ."
Or, better still,
"Once, when I was a little boy . . ."
Or, best of all,
"When Grandfather went to the war . . ."

That was the story where Grandfather lay all day in the tall grass watching for Johnny Reb, and Johnny Reb was watching for Grandfather. When it came to the exciting part, you sat straight up to see Grandfather squint one eye and look along his outstretched arm, as though it were his gun, and say, "Bang!"

But Johnny Reb saw the tip of Grandfather's blue cap just peeping over the tops of the tall grass, and so he, too, went "Bang!"

"YOU STOLE SOFTLY TO HIS SIDE"

Grandfather

And ever afterwards Grandfather walked with a cane.

"Did Johnny Reb have to walk with a cane, too, Grandfather?"

"Johnny Reb, he just lay in the tall grass, all doubled up, and says he, 'Gimme a chaw o' terbaccer afore I die.'"

"Did you give it to him, Grandfather?"

"He died 'fore I could get the plug out o' my pocket."

Then Mother would say:

"I wouldn't, Father—such stories to a child!"

Then Grandfather would smoke grimly, and would not tell you any more, and you would play Grandfather and Johnny Reb in the tall grass. Lizzie-in-the-kitchen would give you a piece of brown-bread for the chaw of tobacco, and when Johnny Reb died too soon you ate it yourself, to save it. You wondered what would

In the Morning Glow

have happened if Johnny Reb had *not* died too soon. Standing over Johnny Reb's prostrate but still animate form in the tall grass, with the brown-bread tobacco in your hand, you even contemplated playing that your adversary lived to tell the tale, but the awful thought that in that case you would have to give up the chaw (the brown-bread was fresh that day) kept you to the letter of Grandfather's story. Once only did you play that Johnny Reb lived — but the brown-bread was hard that day, and you were not hungry.

Grandfather wore the blue, and on his breast were the star and flag of the Grand Army. Every May he straightened his bent shoulders and marched to the music of fife and drum to the cemetery on the hill. So once a year there were tears in Grandfather's eyes. All the rest of that

Grandfather

solemn May day he marched in the garden with his hands behind him, and a far-away look in his eyes, and once in a while his steps quickened as he hummed to himself,

"Tramp, tramp, tramp, the boys are marching."

And if it so happened that he told you the story of Johnny Reb that day, he would always have a new ending:

"Then we went into battle. The Rebs were on a tarnal big hill, and as we charged up the side, 'Boys,' says the Colonel—'boys, give 'em hell!' says he. And, sir, we just did, I tell you."

"Oh, Father, Father—*don't!*—such language before the child!" Mother would cry, and that would be the end of the new end of Grandfather's story.

On a soap-box in Abe Jones's corner grocery, Grandfather argued politics with

In the Morning Glow

Old Man Stubbs and the rest of the boys.

"I've voted the straight Republican ticket all my life," he would say, proudly, when the fray was at its height, "and, by George! I'll not make a darned old fool o' myself by turning coat now. Pesky few Democrats ever I see who—"

Here Old Man Stubbs would rise from the cracker-barrel.

"If I understand you correctly, sir, you have called me a darned old fool."

"Not at all, Stubbs," Grandfather would reply, soothingly. "Not by a jugful. Now you're a Democrat—"

"And proud of it, sir," Old Man Stubbs would break in.

"You're a Democrat, Stubbs, and *as* such you are not responsible; but if I was to turn Democrat, Stubbs, I'd be a darned old fool."

Grandfather

And in the roar that followed, Old Man Stubbs would subside to the cracker-barrel and smoke furiously. Then Grandfather would say:

"Stubbs, do you remember old Mose Gray?" That was to clear the battle-field of the political carnage, so to speak—so that Old Man Stubbs would forget his grievance and walk home with Grandfather peaceably when the grocery closed for the night.

If it was winter-time, and the snow-drifts were too deep for grandfathers and little boys, you sat before the fireplace, Grandfather in his arm-chair, you flat on the rug, your face between your hands, gazing into the flames.

"Who was the greatest man that ever lived, Grandfather?"

"Jesus of Nazareth, boy."

"And who was the greatest soldier?"

In the Morning Glow

"Ulysses S. Grant."

"And the next greatest?"

"George Washington.'

"But Old Man Stubbs says Napoleon was the greatest soldier."

"Old Man Stubbs? Old Man Stubbs? What does he know about it, I'd like to know? He wasn't in the war. He's afraid of his own shadder. U. S. Grant was the greatest general that ever lived. I guess I know. I was there, wasn't I? Napoleon! Old Man Stubbs! Fiddlesticks!"

And Grandfather would sink back into his chair, smoking wrath and weed in his trembling corn-cob, and scowling at the blazing fagots and the curling hickory smoke. By-and-by—

"Who was the greatest woman that ever lived, Grandfather?"

"Your mother, boy."

Grandfather

"Oh, Father"—it was Mother's voice—"you forget."

"Forget nothing," cried Grandfather, fiercely. "Boy, your mother is the best woman that ever lived, and mind you remember it, too. Every boy's mother is the best woman that ever lived."

And when Grandfather leaned forward in his chair and waved his pipe, there was no denying Grandfather.

At night, after supper, when your clothes were in a little heap on the chair, and you had your nighty on, and you had said your prayers, Mother tucked you in bed and kissed you and called Grandfather. Then Grandfather came stumping up the stairs with his cane. Sitting on the edge of your bed, he sang to you,

> "The wild gazelle with the silvery feet
> I'll give thee for a playmate sweet."

In the Morning Glow

And after Grandfather went away the wild gazelle came and stood beside you, and put his cold little nose against your cheek, and licked your face with his tongue. It was rough at first, but by-and-by it got softer and softer, till you woke up and wanted a drink, and found beside you, in place of the wild gazelle, a white mother with a brimming cup in her hand. She covered you up when you were through, and kissed you, and then you went looking for the wild gazelle, and sometimes you found him; but sometimes, when you had just caught up to him and his silvery feet were shining like stars, he turned into Grandfather with his cane.

"Hi, sleepy-head! The dicky-birds are waitin' for you."

And then Grandfather would tickle you in the ribs, and help you on with your

Grandfather

stockings, till it was time for him to sit by the wall in the sun.

When you were naughty, and Mother used the little brown switch that hung over the wood-shed door, Grandfather tramped up and down in the garden, and the harder you hollered, the harder Grandfather tramped. Once when you played the empty flower-pots were not flower-pots at all, but just cannon-balls, and you killed a million Indians with them, Mother showed you the pieces, and the switch descended, and the tears fell, and Grandfather tramped and tramped, and lost the garden-path completely, and stepped on the pansies. Then they shut you up in your own room up-stairs, and you cried till the hiccups came. You heard the dishes rattling on the dining-room table below. They would be eating supper soon, and at one end of the table

In the Morning Glow

in a silver dish there would be a chocolate cake, for Lizzie-in-the-kitchen had baked one that afternoon. You had seen it in the pantry window with your own eyes, while you fired the flower-pots. Now chocolate cake was your favorite, so you hated your bread-and-milk, and fasted and wailed defiantly. Now and then you listened to hear if they pitied and came to you, but they came not, and you moaned and sobbed in the twilight, and hoped you would die, to make them sorry. By-and-by, between the hiccups, you heard the door open softly. Then Grandfather's hand came through the crack with a piece of chocolate cake in it. You knew it was Grandfather's hand, because it was all knuckly. So you cried no more, and while the chocolate cake was stopping the hiccups, you heard Grandfather steal down the stairs, softly—but it did not

Grandfather

sound like Grandfather at all, for you did not hear the stumping of his cane. Next morning, when you asked him about it, his vest shook, and just the tip of his tongue showed between his teeth, for that was the way it did when anything pleased him. And Grandfather said:

"You won't ever tell?"

"No, Grandfather."

"Sure as shootin'?"

"Yes."

"Well, then—" but Grandfather kept shaking so he could not tell.

"Oh, Grandfather! *Why* didn't the cane sound on the stairs?"

"Whisht, boy! I just wrapped my old bandanna handkerchief around the end."

But worse than that time was the awful morning when you broke the blue pitcher that came over in the *Mayflower*. An old family law said you should never even

In the Morning Glow

touch it, where it sat on the shelf by the clock, but the Old Nick said it wouldn't hurt if you looked inside — just once. You had been munching bread-and-butter, and your fingers were slippery, and that is how the pitcher came to fall. Grandfather found you sobbing over the pieces, and his face was white.

"Sonny, Sonny, what have you done?"

"I—I d-didn't mean to, Grandfather."

In trembling fingers Grandfather gathered up the blue fragments—all that was left of the family heirloom, emblem of Mother's ancestral pride.

"'Sh! Don't cry, Sonny. We'll make it all right again."

"M-Moth—Mother 'll whip me."

"'Sh, boy. No, she won't. We'll take it to the tinker. He'll make it all right again. Come."

And you and Grandfather slunk guiltily

"WATCHED HIM MAKE THE BLUE FRAGMENTS
INTO THE BLUE PITCHER AGAIN"

Grandfather

to the tinker and watched him make the blue fragments into the blue pitcher again, and then you carried it home, and as Grandfather set it back on the shelf you whispered:

"Grandfather!"

Grandfather bent his ear to you. Very softly you said it:

"Grandfather, the cracks don't show at all from here."

Grandfather nodded his head. Then he tramped up and down in the garden. He forgot to smoke. Crime weighed upon his soul.

"Boy," said he, sternly, stopping in his walk. "You must never be naughty again. Do you hear me?"

"I won't, Grandfather."

Grandfather resumed his tramping; then paused and turned to where you sat on the wheelbarrow.

In the Morning Glow

"But if you ever *are* naughty again, you must go at once and tell Mother. Do you understand?"

"Yes, Grandfather."

Up and down Grandfather tramped moodily, his head bent, his hands clasped behind him — up and down between the verbenas and hollyhocks. He paused irresolutely—turned—turned again—and came back to you.

"Boy, Grandfather's just as bad and wicked as you are. He ought to have made you tell Mother about the pitcher first, and take it to the tinker afterwards. You must never keep anything from your mother again—*never*. Do you hear?"

"Yes, Grandfather," you whimpered, hanging your head.

"Come, boy."

You gave him your hand. Mother listened, wondering, while Grandfather spoke

Grandfather

out bravely to the very end. You had been bad, but he had been worse, he confessed; and he asked to be punished for himself and you.

Mother did not even look at the cracked blue pitcher on the clock-shelf, but her eyes filled, and at the sight of her tears you flung yourself, sobbing, into her arms.

"Oh, Mother, don't whip Grandfather. Just whip me."

"It isn't the blue pitcher I care about," she said. "It's only to think that Grandfather and my little boy were afraid to tell me."

And at this she broke out crying with your wet cheek against her wet cheek, and her warm arms crushing you to her breast. And you cried, and Grandfather blew his nose, and Carlo barked and leaped to lick your face, until by-and-by, when

In the Morning Glow

Mother's white handkerchief and Grandfather's red one were quite damp, you and Mother smiled through your tears, and she said it did not matter, and Grandfather patted one of her hands while you kissed the other. And you and Grandfather said you would never be bad again.

When you were good, or sick — dear Grandfather! It was not what he said, for only Mother could say the love-words. It was the things he did without saying much at all—the circus he took you to see, the lessons in A B C while he held the book for you in his hand, the sail-boats he whittled for you on rainy days — for Grandfather was a ship-carpenter before he was a grandfather — and the willow whistles he made for you, and the soldier swords. It was Grandfather who fished you from the brook. Grandfather saved you from Farmer Tompkins's cow — the

"THE SAIL-BOATS HE WHITTLED FOR YOU ON RAINY DAYS."

Grandfather

black one which gave no milk. Grandfather snatched you from prowling dogs, and stinging bees, and bad boys and their wiles. That is what grandfathers are for, and so we love them and climb into their laps and beg for sail-boats and tales — and *that* is their reward.

One day—your birthday had just gone by and it was time to think of Thanksgiving—you walked with Grandfather in the fields. Between the stacked corn the yellow pumpkins lay, and they made you think of Thanksgiving pies. The leaves, red and gold, dropped of old age in the autumn stillness, and you gathered an armful for Mother.

"Why don't all the people die every year, Grandfather, like the leaves?"

"Everybody dies when his work's done, little boy. The leaf's work is done in the fall when the frost comes. It takes

In the Morning Glow

longer for a man to do his work, 'cause a man has more to do."

"When will your work be done, Grandfather?"

"It's almost done now, little boy."

"Oh no, Grandfather. There's lots for you to do. You said you'd make me a bob-sled, and a truly engine what goes, when I'm bigger; and when I get to be a grown-up man like Father, you are to come and make willow whistles for *my* little boys."

And you were right, for while the frost came again and again for the little leaves, Grandfather stayed on in the sun, and when he had made you the bob-sled he still lingered, for did he not have the truly engine to make for you, and the willow whistles for your own little boys?

Waking from a nap, you could not remember when you fell asleep. You won-

Grandfather

dered what hour it was. Was it morning? Was it afternoon? Dreamily you came down-stairs. Golden sunlight crossed the ivied porch and smiled at you through the open door. The dining-room table was set with blue china, and at every place was a dish of red, red strawberries. Then you knew it was almost supper-time. You were rested with sleep, gentle with dreams of play, happy at the thought of red berries in blue dishes with sugar and cream. You found Grandfather in the garden sitting in the sun. He was not reading or smoking; he was just waiting.

"Are you tired waiting for me, Grandfather?"

"No, little boy."

"I came as soon as I could, Grandfather."

The leaves did not move. The flowers

In the Morning Glow

were motionless. Grandfather sat quite still, his soft, white beard against your cheek, flushed with sleep. You nestled in his lap. And so you sat together, with the sun going down about you, till Mother came and called you to supper. Even now when you are grown, you remember, as though it were yesterday, the long nap and the golden light in the doorway, and the red berries on the table, and Grandfather waiting in the sun.

One day—it was not long afterwards—they took you to see Aunt Mary, on the train. When you came home again, Grandfather was not waiting for you.

"Where is Grandfather?"

"Grandfather isn't here any more, dearie. He has gone 'way up in the sky to see God and the angels."

"And won't he ever come back to our house?"

Grandfather

"No, dear; but if you are a good boy, you will go to see him some day."

"But, oh, Mother, what will Grandfather do when he goes to walk with the little boy angels? See — he's gone and forgot his cane!"

Grandmother

Grandmother

IN the days when you went into the country to visit her, Grandmother was a gay, spry little lady with velvety cheeks and gold-rimmed spectacles, knitting reins for your hobby-horse, and spreading bread-and-butter and brown sugar for you in the hungry middle of the afternoon. For a bumped head there was nothing in the bottles to compare with the magic of her lips.

"And what did the floor do to my poor little lamb? See! Grandmother will make the place well again." And when she

In the Morning Glow

had kissed it three times, lo! you knew that you were hungry, and on the doorsill of Grandmother's pantry you shed a final tear.

When you arrived for a visit, and Grandmother had taken off your cap and coat as you sat in her lap, you would say, softly, "Grandmother." Then she would know that you wanted to whisper, and she would lower her ear till it was even with your lips. Through the hollow of your two hands you said it:

"I think I would like some sugar pie now, Grandmother."

And then she would laugh till the tears came, and wipe her spectacles, for that was just what she had been waiting for you to say all the time, and if you had not said it—but, of course, that was impossible. Always, on the day before you came, she made two little sugar pies in

Grandmother

two little round tins with crinkled edges. One was for you, and the other was for Lizbeth.

After you had eaten your pies you chased the rooster till he dropped you a white tail-feather in token of surrender, and just tucking the feather into your cap made you an Indian. Grandmother stood at the window and watched you while you scalped the sunflowers. The Indians and tigers at Grandmother's were wilder than those in Our Yard at home.

Being an Indian made you think of tents, and then you remembered Grandmother's old plaid shawl. She never wore it now, for she had a new one, but she kept it for you in the closet beneath the stairs. While you were gone, it hung in the dark alone, dejected, waiting for you to come back and play. When you came, at last, and dragged it forth, it clung to

In the Morning Glow

you warmly, and did everything you said: stretched its frayed length from chair to chair and became a tent for you; swelled proudly in the summer gale till your boat scudded through the surf of waving grass, and you anchored safely, to fish with string and pin, by the Isles of the Red Geraniums.

"The pirates are coming," you cried to Lizbeth, scanning the horizon of picket fence.

"The pirates are coming," she repeated, dutifully.

"And now we must haul up the anchor," you commanded, dragging in the stone. Lizbeth was in terror. "Oh, my poor dolly!" she cried, hushing it in her arms. Gallantly the old plaid shawl caught the breeze; and as it filled, your boat leaped forward through—

"Harry! Lizbeth! Come and be washed for dinner!"

"YOU CLUNG TO HER APRON FOR SUPPORT IN YOUR MUTE AGONY"

Grandmother

Grandmother's voice came out to you across the waters. You hesitated. The pirate ship was close behind. You could see the cutlasses flashing in the sun.

"More sugar pies," sang the Grandmother siren on the rocks of the front porch, and at those melting words the pirate ship was a mere speck on the horizon. Seizing Lizbeth by the hand, you ran boldly across the sea.

By the white bowl Grandmother took your chin in one hand and lifted your face.

"My, what a dirty boy!"

With the rough wet rag she mopped the dirt away — grime of your long sea-voyage — while you squinted your eyes and pursed up your lips to keep out the soap. You clung to her apron for support in your mute agony.

"Grand—" you managed to sputter

In the Morning Glow

ere the wet rag smothered you. Warily you waited till the cloth went higher, to your puckered eyes. Then, "Grand-m-m—" But that was all, for with a trail of suds the rag swept down again, and as the half-word slipped out, the soap slipped in. So Grandmother dug and dug till she came to the pink stratum of your cheeks, and then it was wipe, wipe, wipe, till the stratum shone. Then it was your hands' turn, while Grandmother listened to your belated tale, and last of all she kissed you above and gave you a little spank below, and you were done.

All through dinner your mind was on the table—not on the middle of it, where the meat was, but on the end of it.

"Harry, why don't you eat your bread?"

"Why, I don't feel for bread, Grandmother," you explained, looking at the end of the table. "I just feel for pie."

Grandmother

It was hard when you were back home again, for there it was mostly bread, and no sugar pies at all, and very little cake.

"Grandmother lets me have *two* pieces," you would urge to Mother, but the argument was of no avail. Two pieces, she said, were not good for little boys.

"Then why does Grandmother let me have them?" you would demand, sullenly, kicking the table leg; but Mother could not hear you unless you kicked hard, and then it was naughty boys, not Grandmothers, that she talked about. And if that happened which sometimes does to naughty little boys—

"Grandmother don't hurt at all when *she* spanks," you said.

So there were wrathful moments when you wished you might live always with Grandmother. It was so easy to be good at her house—so easy, that is, to get two

In the Morning Glow

pieces of cake. And when God made little boys, you thought, He must have made Grandmothers to bake sugar pies for them.

"Suppose you were a little boy like me, Grandmother?" you once said to her.

"That would be fine," she admitted; "but suppose you were a little grandmother like me?"

"Well," you replied, with candor, "I think I would rather be like Grandfather, 'cause he was a soldier, and fought Johnny Reb."

"And if you were a grandfather," Grandmother asked, "what would you do?"

"Why, if I were a grandfather," you said—"why—"

"Well, what would you do?"

"Why, if I were a grandfather," you said, "I should want you to come and be a grandmother with me." And Grandmother kissed you for that.

Grandmother

"But I like you best as a little boy," she said. "Once Grandmother had a little boy just like you, and he used to climb into her lap and put his arms around her. Oh, he was a beautiful little boy, and sometimes Grandmother gets very lonesome without him — till you come, and then it's like having him back again. For you've got his blue eyes and his brown hair and his sweet little ways, and Grandmother loves you — once for yourself and once for him."

"But where is the little boy now, Grandmother?"

"He's a man now, darling. He's your own father."

Every Sunday, Grandmother went to church. After breakfast there was a flurry of dressing, with an opening and shutting of doors up-stairs, and Grandfather would be down-stairs in the kitchen, blacking

In the Morning Glow

his Sunday boots. On Sunday his beard looked whiter than on other days, but that was because he seemed so much blacker everywhere else. He creaked out to the stable and hitched Peggy to the buggy and led them around to the front gate. Then he would snap his big gold watch and go to the bottom of the stairs and say:

"Maria! Come! It's ten o'clock."

Grandmother's door would open a slender crack — "Yes, John" — and Grandfather would creak up and down in his Sunday boots, up and down, waiting, till there was a rustling on the stairs and Grandmother came down to him in a glory of black silk. There was a little frill of white about her neck, fastened with her gold brooch, and above that her gentle Sabbath face. Her face took on a new light when Sunday came, and she never

"YOU WATCHED THEM AS THEY WENT DOWN THE WALK TOGETHER"

Grandmother

seemed so near, somehow, as on other days. There was a look in her eyes that did not speak of sugar pies or play. There was a little pressure of the thin lips and a silence, as though she had no time for fairy-tales or lullabies. When she set her little black bonnet on her gray hair and lifted up her chin to tie the ribbon strings beneath, you stopped your game to watch, wondering at her awesomeness; and when in her black-gloved fingers she clasped her worn Bible and stooped and kissed you good-bye, you never thought of putting your arms around her. She was too wonderful — this little Sabbath Grandmother—for that.

Through the window you watched them as they went down the walk together to the front gate, Grandmother and Grandfather, the tips of her gloved fingers laid in the hollow of his arm. Solemn was

In the Morning Glow

the steady stumping of his cane. Solemn was the day. Even the roosters knew it was Sunday, somehow, and crowed dismally; and the bells—the church-bells tolling through the quiet air—made you lonesome and cross with Lizbeth. Your collar was very stiff, and your Sunday trousers were very tight, and there was nothing to do, and you were dreary.

After dinner Grandfather went to sleep on the sofa, with a newspaper over his face. Then Grandmother took you up into her black silk lap and read you Bible stories and taught you the Twenty-third Psalm and the golden text. And every one of the golden texts meant the same thing — that little boys should be very good and do as they are told.

Grandmother's Sunday lap was not so fine as her other ones to lie in. Her Monday lap, for instance, was soft and gray,

Grandmother

and there were no texts to disturb your reverie. Then Grandmother would stop her knitting to pinch your cheek and say, "You don't love Grandmother."

"Yes, I do."

"How much?"

"More'n tonguecantell. What is a tonguecantell, Grandmother?"

And while she was telling you she would be poking the tip of her finger into the soft of your jacket, so that you doubled up suddenly with your knees to your chin; and while you guarded your ribs a funny spider would crawl down the back of your neck; and when you chased the spider out of your collar it would suddenly creep under your chin, or there would be a panic in the ribs again. By that time you were nothing but wriggles and giggles and little cries.

"Don't, Grandmother; you tickle." And

In the Morning Glow

Grandmother would pause, breathless as yourself, and say, "*Oh*, my!"

"Now you must do it some more, Grandmother," you would urge, but she would shake her head at you and go back to her knitting again.

"Grandmother's tired," she would say.

You were tired, too, so you lay with your head on her shoulder, sucking your thumb. To and fro Grandmother rocked you, to and fro, while the kitten played with the ball of yarn on the floor. The afternoon sunshine fell warmly through the open window. Bees and butterflies hovered in the honeysuckles. Birds were singing. Your mind went a-wandering—out through the yard and the front gate and across the road. On it went past the Taylors' big dog and up by Aunty Green's, where the crullers lived, all brown and crusty, in the high stone crock. It

"TO AND FRO GRANDMOTHER ROCKED YOU"

Grandmother

scrambled down by the brook where the little green frogs were hopping into the water, leaving behind them trembling rings that grew wider and wider and wider, till pretty soon they were the ocean. That was a big thought, and you roused yourself.

"How big is the ocean, Grandmother?"

"As big—oh, as big as all out-doors."

Your mind waded out into the ocean till the water was up to its knees. Then it scrambled back again and lay in the warm sand and looked up at the sky. And the sand rocked to and fro, to and fro, as your mind lay there, all curled up and warm, by the ocean, watching the butterflies in the honeysuckles and the crullers in the crock. And all the people were singing . . . all the people in the world, almost . . . and the little green frogs. . . . "Bye—bye, bye—bye," they were singing, in time to the rocking of

In the Morning Glow

the sand . . . "Bye — bye" . . . "Bye" . . . "Bye" . . .

And when you awoke you were on the sofa, all covered up with Grandmother's shawl.

So you liked the gay week-day Grandmother best, with her soft lap and her lullabies. Grandfather must have liked her best too, you thought, for when he went away forever and forgot his cane, it was the Sunday Grandmother he left behind—a little, gray Grandmother sitting by the window and gazing silently through the panes.

What she saw there you never knew—but it was not the trees, or the distant hills, or the people passing in the road.

While Aunt Jane Played

While Aunt Jane Played

AUNT JANE played the piano in the parlor. You could play, too—"Peter, Peter, Punkin-eater," with your forefinger, Aunt Jane holding it in her hand so that you would strike the right notes. But when Aunt Jane played she used both hands. Sometimes the music was so fast and stirring that it made you dance, or romp, or sing, or play that you were not a little boy at all, but a soldier like Grandfather or George Washington; and sometimes the music was so soft and beautiful that you wanted to be a prince in a

In the Morning Glow

fairy tale; and then again it was so slow and grim that you wished it were not Sunday, for the Sunday tunes, like your tight, black, Sunday shoes, had all their buttons on, and so were not comfy or made for fun. You could not march to them, or fight to them, or be a grown-up man to them. Somehow they always reminded you that you were only a pouting, naughty little boy.

The sound of the piano came out to you as you lingered by the table where Lizzie-in-the-kitchen was making pies. You ran into the parlor and sat on a hassock by Aunt Jane, watching her as she played. It was not a fast piece that day, nor yet a slow one, but just in-between, so that as you sat by the piano you wondered if the snow and sloppy little puddles would ever go and leave Our Yard green again. Even with rubber boots now Mother made

While Aunt Jane Played

you keep the paths, and mostly you had to stay in the house. Through the window you could see the maple boughs still bare, but between them the sky was warm and blue. Pretty soon the leaves would be coming, hiding the sky.

"Auntie."

"Yes," though she did not stop playing.

"Where do the leaves come from?"

"From the little buds on the twigs, dearie."

"But how do they know when it's time to come, Auntie Jane? 'Cause if they came too soon, they might catch cold and die."

"Well, the sun tells them when."

"How does the sun tell them, Auntie?"

"Why, he makes the trees all warm, and when the buds feel it, out they come."

"Oh."

Your eyes were very wide. They were

In the Morning Glow

always wide when you wondered; and sometimes when you were not wondering at all, just hearing Aunt Jane play would make you, and then your eyes would grow bigger and bigger as you sat on the hassock by the piano, looking at the maple boughs and hearing the music and being a little boy.

It was a beautiful piece that Aunt Jane was playing that March morning. The sun came and shone on the maple boughs.

"And now the sun is telling the little buds," you said to yourself in time to Aunt Jane's music, but so softly that she did not hear.

"And now the little buds are saying 'All right,'" you whispered, more softly still, for the bigger your eyes got, the smaller, always, was your voice.

A little song-sparrow came and teetered on a twig.

While Aunt Jane Played

"Oh, Auntie, see! The birdie's come, too, to tell the buds, I guess."

Aunt Jane turned her head and smiled at the sparrow, but she did not stop playing. Your heart was beating in time to the music, as you sat on the hassock by the piano, watching the bird and the sun. The sparrow danced like Aunt Jane's fingers, and put up his little open bill. He was singing, though you could not hear.

"But, Auntie."

"Yes."

"Who told the little bird?"

"God told the little bird, dearie—away down South where the oranges and roses grow in the winter, and there isn't any snow. And the little bird flew up here to Ourtown to build his nest and sing in our maple-tree."

Your eyes were so wide now that you

In the Morning Glow

had no voice at all. You just sat there on the hassock while Aunt Jane played.

Away down South . . . away down South, singing in an orange-tree, you saw the little bird . . . but now he stopped to listen with his head on one side, and his bright eye shining, while the warm wind rustled in the leaves . . . God was telling him . . . So the little bird spread his wings and flew . . . away up in the blue sky, above the trees, above the steeples, over the hills and running brooks . . . miles and miles and miles . . . till he came to Our Yard, in the sun.

"And here he is now," you ended aloud your little story, for you had found your voice again.

"Who is here, dearie?" asked Aunt Jane, still playing.

"Why, the little bird," you said.

The sparrow flew away. The sun came

While Aunt Jane Played

through the window to where you sat on the hassock, by the piano. It warmed your knees and told you — what it told the buds, what God told the little bird in the orange-tree. Like the little bird you could stay no longer. You ran out-of-doors into the soft, sweet wind and the morning.

Aunt Jane gave the keys a last caress. Grandmother turned in her chair by the sitting-room window.

"What were you playing, Janey?"

"Mendelssohn's 'Spring Song,' Mother."

The little gray Grandmother looked out-of-doors again to where you played, singing, in the sun.

"Isn't it beautiful?" she murmured.

You waved your hand to her and laughed, and she nodded back at you, smiling at your fun.

"Bless his heart, *he's* playing the music, too," she said.

Little Sister

Little Sister

IN the daytime she played with you, and believed all you said, and was always ready to cry. At night she slept with you and the four dolls. She was your little sister, Lizbeth.

"Whose little girl are you?" they would ask her. If she were sitting in Father's lap, she would doubtless reply—

"Father's little girl."

But—

"Oh, *Lizbeth!*" Mother would cry.

"—and Mother's," Lizbeth would add, to keep peace in the family. Though she

In the Morning Glow

never mentioned you at such times, she told you privately that she would marry you when you grew to be a man, and publicly she remembered you in her prayers. Kneeling down at Mother's knee, you and Lizbeth, in your little white nighties, before you went to bed, you said "Now I lay me" in unison, and ended with blessing every one, only at the very end *you* said:

"—and God bless Captain Jinks," for even a wooden soldier needed God in those long, dark nights of childhood, while Lizbeth said:

"—and God bless all my dollies, and send my Sally doll a new leg."

But though God sent three new legs in turn, Sally was always losing them, so that finally Lizbeth confided in Mother:

"Pretty soon God 'll be tired of sending Sally new legs, I guess. *You* speak

"YOU SAID 'NOW I LAY ME' IN UNISON"

Little Sister

to Him next time, Mother, 'cause I'm 'shamed to any more."

And when Mother asked Him, He sent a new Sally instead of a new leg. It would be cheaper, Mother told Father, in the long-run.

In the diplomatic precedence of Lizbeth's prayers, Father and Mother were blessed first, and you came between "Grandfather and Grandmother" and "God bless my dollies." Thus was your family rank established for all time by a little girl in a white night-gown. You were a little lower than your elders, it is true, but you were higher than the legless Sally or the waxen blonde.

When Lizbeth and you were good, you loved each other, and when you were bad, both of you at the same time, you loved **each** other too, *very* dearly. But sometimes it happened that Lizbeth was **good**

In the Morning Glow

and you were bad, and then she only loved Mother, and ran and told tales on you. And you—well, you did not love anybody at all.

When your insides said it would be a long time before dinner, and your mouth watered, and you stood on a chair by the pantry shelf with your hand in a brown jar, and when Lizbeth found you there, you could tell by just looking at her face that she was very good that day, and that she loved Mother better than she did you. So you knew without even thinking about it that you were very bad, and you did not love anybody at all, and your heart quaked within you at Lizbeth's sanctity. But there was always a last resort.

"Lizbeth, if you tell"—you mumbled awfully, pointing at her an uncanny forefinger dripping preserves—"if you tell, a great big black Gummy-gum 'll get you

Little Sister

when it's dark, and he'll pick out your eyes and gnaw your ears off, and he'll keep one paw over your mouth, so you can't holler, and when the blood comes—"

Lizbeth quailed before you. She began to cry.

"You won't tell, *will* you?" you demanded, fiercely, making eyes like a Gummy-gum and showing your white teeth.

"No—o—o," wailed Lizbeth.

"Well, stop crying, then," you commanded, sucking your syrupy fingers. "If you cry, the Gummy-gum 'll come and get you *now*."

Lizbeth looked fearfully over her shoulder and stopped. By that time your fingers were all sucked, and the cover was back on the jar, and you were saved. But that night, when Mother and Father came home, you watched Lizbeth, and lest she should

In the Morning Glow

forget, you made the eyes of a Gummy-gum, when no one but Lizbeth saw. Mother tucked you both into bed and kissed you and put out the light. Then Lizbeth whimpered.

"Why, Lizbeth," said Mother from the dark.

Quick as a flash you snuggled up to Lizbeth's side. "The Gummy-gum 'll get you if you don't stop," you whispered, warningly—but with one dismal wail Lizbeth was out of bed and in Mother's arms. Then you knew all was over. Desperately you awaited retribution, humming a little song, and so it was to the tune of "I want to be an angel" that you heard Lizbeth sob out her awful tale:

"Harry . . . he . . . he said the Gummy-gum 'd get me . . . if I told about the p'serves."

And it was *you* the Gummy-gum got

Little Sister

that time, and your blood, you thought, almost came.

But other nights when you went to bed — nights after days when you had both been good and loved each other—it was fine to lie there in the dark with Lizbeth, playing Make-Believe before you fell asleep.

"I tell you," you said, putting up your foot so that the covers rose upon it, making a little tent—"I tell you; let's be Indians."

"Let's," said Lizbeth.

"And this is our little tent, and there's bears outside what 'll eat you up if you don't look out."

Lizbeth shivered and drew her knees up to her chin, so that she was nothing but a little warm roll under the wigwam.

"And now the bears are coming—wow! wow! wow!"

And as the great hungry beasts push-

In the Morning Glow

ed their snouts under the canvas and growled and gnashed their teeth, Lizbeth, little squaw, squealed with terror, and seized you as you lay there helpless in your triple rôle of tent and bears and Indian brave; seized you in the ticklish ribs so that the wigwam came tumbling about your ears, and the Indian brave rolled and shrieked with laughter, and the brute bears fled to their mountain caves.

"Children!"

"W—what?"

"Stop that noise and go right to sleep. Do you hear me?"

Was it not the voice of the mamma bear? Stealthily you crept under the fallen canvas, which had grown smaller, somehow, in the *mêlée*, so that when you pulled it up to your chin and tucked it in around you, Lizbeth was out in the cold; and when Lizbeth tucked herself in, then you

"MOTHER TUCKED YOU BOTH INTO BED AND KISSED YOU"

Little Sister

were shivering. But by-and-by you huddled close in the twisted sheets and talked low beneath the edge of the coverlet, so that no one heard you—not even the Gummy-gum, who spent his nights on the back stairs.

"Does the Gummy-gum eat little folks while they're asleep?" asked Lizbeth, with a precautionary snuggle-up.

"No; 'cause the Gummy-gum is afraid of the little black gnomes what live in the pillows."

"Well, if the little black gnomes live in the pillows, why can't you feel them then?"

"'Cause, now, they're so teenty-weenty and so soft."

"And can't you ever see them at all?"

"No; 'cause they don't come out till you're asleep."

"Oh . . . Well, Harry — now — if a

In the Morning Glow

Gummy-gum had a head like a horse, and a tail like a cow, and a bill like a duck, what?"

"Why — why, he *wouldn't*, 'cause he *isn't*."

"Oh . . . Well, is the Gummy-gum just afraid of the little gnomes, and that's all?"

"Um-hm; 'cause the little gnomes have little knives, all sharp and shiny, what they got on the Christmas-tree."

"*Our* Christmas-tree?"

"No; the little gnomes's Christmas-tree."

"The little gnomes's Christmas-tree?"

"Um-hm."

"Why?"

"'Cause . . . why, there ain't any why . . . just Christmas-tree."

"Just . . . just Christmas-tree?"

"Um."

"Why . . . I thought . . . I . . ."

And you and Lizbeth never felt Mother

Little Sister

smooth out the covers at all, though she lifted you up to straighten them; and so you slept, spoon-fashion, warm as toast, with the little black gnomes watching in the pillows, and the Gummy-gum, hungry but afraid, in the dark of the back stairs.

The pear-tree on the edge of the enchanted garden, green with summer and tremulous with breeze, sheltered a little girl and her dolls. On the cool turf she sat alone, preoccupied, her dress starched and white like the frill of a valentine, her fat little legs straight out before her, her bright little curls straight down behind, her lips parted, her eyes gentle with a dream of motherhood — Mamma Lizbeth crooning lullabies to her four children cradled in the soft grass.

"I'll tell you just one more story," she was saying, "just one, and that's all, and then you children must go to sleep. Sally,

In the Morning Glow

lie still! Ain't you 'shamed, kicking all the covers off and catching cold? Naughty girl. Now you must listen. Well . . . Once upon a time there was a fairy what lived in a rose, and she had beautiful wings —oh, all colors—and she could go wherever she wanted to without anybody ever seeing her, 'cause she was iwisible, which is when you can't see anybody at all. Well, one day the fairy saw a little girl carrying her father's dinner, and she turned herself into an old witch and said to the little girl, 'Come to me, pretty one, and I will give thee a stick of peppermint candy.' Now the little girl, she just loved candy, and peppermint was her favorite, but she was a good little girl and minded her mother most dut'fly, and never told any lies or anything; so she courtesied to the old witch and said, 'Thank you kindly, but I must hurry with my father's dinner, or he will

Little Sister

be hungry waiting.' *And what do you think?* Just then the old witch turned into the beautiful fairy again, and she kissed the little girl, and gave her a whole bag of peppermint candy, and a doll what talked, and a velocipede for her little brother. And what does this story teach us, children? . . . Yes. That's right. It teaches us to be good little boys and girls and mind our parents. And that's all."

The dolls fell asleep. Lizbeth whispered lest they should awake, and tiptoed through the grass. A blue-jay called harshly from a neighboring tree. Lizbeth frowned and glanced anxiously at the grassy trundle-bed. " 'Sh!" she said, warningly, her finger on her lip, whenever you came near.

Suddenly there was a rustle in the leaves above, and out of their greenness a little pear dropped to the grass at Lizbeth's feet.

In the Morning Glow

"It's mine," you cried, reaching out your hand.

"No—o," screamed Lizbeth. "It's for my dollies' breakfast," and she hugged the stunted, speckled fruit to her bosom so tightly that its brown, soft side was crushed in her hands. You tried to snatch it from her, but she struck you with her little clinched fist.

"No—o," she cried again. "It's my dollies' pear." Her lip quivered. Tears sprang into her eyes. You straightened yourself.

"All right," you muttered, fiercely. "All right for you. I'll run away, I will, and I'll never come back—*never!*"

You climbed the stone wall.

"No," cried Lizbeth.

"I'll never come back," you called, defiantly, as you stood on the top.

"No," Lizbeth screamed, scrambling to

Little Sister

her feet and turning to you a face wet with tears and white with terror.

"Never, *never!*" was your farewell to her as you jumped. Deaf to the pitiful wail behind you, you ran out across the meadow, muttering to yourself your fateful, parting cry.

Lizbeth looked for a moment at the wall where you had stood. Then she ran sobbing after you, around through the gate, for the wall was too high for her, and out into the field, where to her blurred vision you were only a distant figure now, never, never to return.

"Harry!" she screamed, and the wind blew her cry to you across the meadow, but you ran on, unheeding. She struggled after you. The daisies brushed her skirt. Creeping vines caught at her little shoes and she fell. Scratched by briers, she scrambled to her feet again and stum-

In the Morning Glow

bled on, blind with tears, crying ever "Harry, Harry!" but so faintly now in her sobs and breathlessness that you did not hear. At the top of a weary, weary slope she sank helpless and heartbroken in the grass, a little huddle of curls and pinafore, so that your conscience smote you as you stood waiting, half hidden by the hedge.

"Don't be a cry-baby. I was only fooling," you said, and at the sound of your voice Lizbeth lifted her face from the grasses and put out her arms to you with a cry. In one hand was the little pear.

"Oh, I don't want the old thing," you cried, throwing yourself beside her on the turf. Smiling again through her tears, Lizbeth reached out a little hand scratched by briers, and patted your cheek.

"Harry," she said, "you can have all my animal crackers for your m'nagerie, if you want to, and my little brown don-

Little Sister

key; and I'll play horse with you *any* time you want me to, Harry, I will."

So, after all, you did not run away, and you and Lizbeth went home at last across the meadow, hand in hand. Behind you, hidden and forgotten in the red clover, lay your quarrel and the little pear.

When Lizbeth loved you, there were stars in her brown eyes; when you looked more closely, so that you were very near their shining, you saw in their round, black pupils, smiling back at you, the face of a little boy; and then in your own eyes, Lizbeth, holding your cheeks between her hands, found the face of a little girl.

"Why, it's *me!*" she cried.

And when you looked again into Lizbeth's eyes, you saw yourself; and "Oh, Mother," you said afterwards, for you had thought deeply, "I think it's the *good*

In the Morning Glow

Harry that's in Lizbeth's eyes, 'cause when I look at him, he's always smiling." That was as far as you thought about it then; but once, long afterwards, it came to you that little boys never find their pictures in a sister's eyes unless they are good, and love her, and hold her cheeks between their hands.

Lizbeth's cheeks were softer than yours, and when she played horse, or the day was windy, so that the grass rippled and the trees sang, or when it was tub-day with soap and towels up-stairs, her cheeks were pink as the roses in Mother's garden. That is how you came to tell Mother a great secret, one evening in summer, as you sat with her and Lizbeth on the front steps watching the sun go down.

"I guess it's tub-day in the sky, Mother."

"Tub-day?"

"Why, yes. All the little clouds have

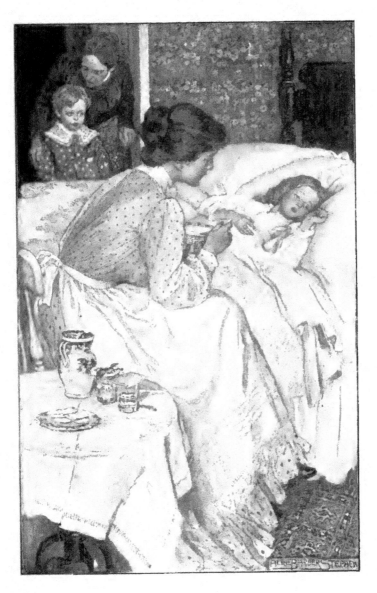

"THEY TOOK YOU AS FAR AS THE BEDROOM
DOOR TO SEE HER"

Little Sister

been having their bath, I think, 'cause they're all pink and shiny, like Lizbeth."

But once Lizbeth's cheeks were white, and she stayed in bed every day, and you played by yourself. Twice a day they took you as far as the bedroom door to see her.

"H'lo," you said, as you peeked.

"H'lo," she whispered back, very softly, for she was almost asleep, and she did not even smile at you, and before you could tell her what the Pussy-cat did they took you away—but not till you had seen the two glasses on the table with the silver spoon on top.

There was no noise in the days then. Even the trees stopped singing, and the wind walked on tiptoe and whispered into people's ears, like you.

"Is it to-day Lizbeth comes down-stairs?" you asked every morning.

In the Morning Glow

"Do you think Lizbeth will play with me to-morrow?" you asked every night. Night came a long time after morning in the days when Lizbeth could not play.

"Oh, dear, I don't think I feel very well," you told Mother. Tears spilled out of your eyes and rolled down your cheeks. Mother felt your brow and looked at your tongue.

"*I* know what's the matter with my little boy," she said, and kissed you; but she did not put you to bed.

One day, when no one was near, you peeked and saw Lizbeth. She was alone and very little and very white.

"H'lo," you said.

"H'lo," she whispered back, and smiled at you, and when she smiled you could not wait any longer. You went in very softly and kissed her where she lay and

Little Sister

gave her a little hug. She patted your cheek.

"I'd like my dollies," she whispered. You brought them to her, all four—the two china ones and the rag brunette and the waxen blonde.

"Dollies are sick," she said. "They 'most died, I guess. Play you're sick, too."

Mother found you there—Lizbeth and you and the four dolls, side by side on the bed, all in a little sick row. And from the very moment that you kissed Lizbeth and gave her the little hug, she grew better, so that by-and-by the wind blew louder and the trees sang lustily, and all Our Yard was bright with flowers and sun and voices and play, for you and Lizbeth and the four dolls were well again.

Our Yard

Our Yard

THE breadth of Our Yard used to be from the beehives to the red geraniums. When the beehives were New York, the geraniums were Japan, so the distance is easy to calculate. The apple-tree Alps overshadowed New York then, which seems strange now, but geography is not what it used to be. In the lapse of years the Manhattan hives have crumbled in the Alpine shade, an earthquake of garden spade has wiped Japan from the map, and where the scarlet islands lay in the sun there are green billows now, and other little boys in the grass, at play.

In the Morning Glow

In the old days when you sailed away on the front gate, which swung and creaked through storms, to the other side of the sea, you could just descry through a fog of foliage the rocky shores of the back-yard fence, washed by a surf of golden-rod. If you moored your ship—for an unlatched gate meant prowling dogs in the garden, and Mother was cross at that—if you anchored your gate-craft dutifully to become a soldier, you could march to the back fence, but it was a long journey. Starting, a drummer-boy, you could never foretell your end, for the future was vague, even with the fence in view, and your cocked hat on your curls, and your drumsticks in your hand. Lizbeth and the dolls might halt you at the front steps and muster you out of service to become a doctor with Grandmother's spectacles and Grandfather's cane. And if

Our Yard

the dolls were well that day, with normal pulses and unflushed cheeks, and you marched by with martial melody, there was your stalled hobby-horse on the side porch, neighing to you for clover hay; and stopping to feed him meant desertion from the ranks, to become a farmer, tilling the soil and bartering acorn eggs and clean sand butter on market-day. And even though you marched untempted by bucolic joys, there lay in wait for you the kitchen door, breathing a scent of crullers, or gingerbread, or apple-pies, or leading your feet astray to the unscraped frosting-bowl or the remnant cookies burned on one side, and so not good for supper, but fine for weary drummer-boys. So whether you reached the fence that day was a question for you and the day and the sirens that beckoned to you along your play.

In the Morning Glow

Across the clover prairie the trellis mountains reared their vine-clad heights. Through their morning-glories ran a little pass, which led to the enchanted garden on the other side, but the pass was so narrow and overhung with vines that when Grandfather was a pack-horse and carried you through on his back, your outstretched feet would catch on the trellis sides. Then the pack-horse would pick his way cautiously and you would dig your heels into his sides and hold fast, and so you got through. Once inside the garden, oh, wonder of pansies and hollyhocks and bachelor's-buttons and roses and sweet smells! The sun shone warmest there, and the fairies lived there, Mother said.

"But when it rains, Mother?"

"Oh, then they hide beneath the trellis, under the honeysuckles."

Mother wore an apron and sun-bonnet,

Our Yard

and knelt in the little path, digging with a trowel in the moist, brown earth. You helped her with your little spade. Under a lilac-bush Lizbeth made mud-pies, and the pies of the enchanted garden were the brownest and richest in all Our Yard. They were the most like Mother's, Lizbeth said. Grandfather sat on the wheelbarrow-ship and smoked.

"Do fairies smoke, Grandfather?"

"The old grandfather fairies do," he said.

Of all the flowers in the enchanted garden you liked the roses best, and of all the roses you liked the red. There was a big one that hung on the wall above your head. You could just reach it when you stood on tiptoe, and pulling it down to you then, you would bury your face in its petals and take a long snuff, and say,

"Um-m-m."

In the Morning Glow

And when you let it go, it bobbed and courtesied on its prickly stem. But one morning, very early, when you pulled it down to you, you were rough with it, and it sprinkled your face with dew.

"The rose is crying," Lizbeth said.

"You should be very gentle with roses," Mother told you. "Sometimes when folks are sick or cross, just the sight of a red rose cheers them and makes them smile again."

That was a beautiful thought, and it came back to you the day you left Our Yard and ran away. You were gone a long time. It was late in the afternoon when you trudged guiltily back again, and when you were still a long way off you could see Mother waiting for you at the gate. The brown switch, doubtless, was waiting too. So you stole into Our Yard through the back fence, and hid

Our Yard

in the enchanted garden, crying and afraid. It began to rain, a gentle summer shower, and like the fairies you hid beneath the honeysuckles. Looking up through your tears, you saw the red rose—and remembered. The rain stopped. You climbed upon the wheelbarrow-ship and pulled the rose from the vine. Trembling, you approached the house. Softly you opened the front door. At the sight of you Mother gave a little cry. Your lip quivered; the tears rolled down your cheeks; for you were cold and wet and dreary.

"M-mother," you said, with outstretched hand, "here's a r-rose I brought you"; and she folded you and the flower in her arms. It was true, then, what she had told you—that when people are cross there is sometimes nothing in the world like the sight of a sweet red rose to cheer them and make them smile again.

In the Morning Glow

Once in Our Yard, you were safe from bad boys and their fists, from bad dogs and their bites, and all the other perils of the road. Yet Our Yard had its dangers too. Through the rhubarb thicket in the corner of the fence stalked a black bear. You had heard him growl. You had seen the flash of his white teeth. You had tracked him to his lair. Just behind you, one hand upon your coat, came Lizbeth.

"'Sh! I see him," you whispered, as you raised your wooden gun.

Bang! Bang!

And the bear fell dead.

"Don't hurt Pussy," said Mother, warningly.

"No," you said, and the dead bear purred and rubbed his head against your legs. Once, after you had killed and eaten him, he mewed and ran before you

Our Yard

to his basket-cave; and there were five little bears, all blind and crying, and you took them home and tamed them by the kitchen fire.

But the bear was nothing to the Wild Man who lived next door. In the barn, close to your fence, he lay in wait for little girls and boys to eat them and drink their blood and gnaw their bones. Oh, you had seen him once yourself, as you peered through a knot-hole in the barn-side. He was sitting on an upturned water-pail, smoking a pipe and muttering.

You and Lizbeth stole out to look at him. Hand in hand you tiptoed across the clover prairie where the red Indians roved. You scanned the horizon, but there was not a feather or painted face in sight to-day — though they always came when you least expected them, popping up from the tall grass with wild, blood-curdling

In the Morning Glow

yells, and scalping you when you didn't watch out. Across the prairie, then, you went, silently, hand in hand. The sun fell warm and golden in the open. Birds were singing in the sky, unmindful of the lurking perils among the tall grass and beyond the fence. Back of you were home and Mother's arms, and in the pantry window, cooling, two juicy pies. Before you, across the clover, a great gray dungeon frowned upon you; within its walls a creature of blood and mystery waiting with hungry jaws. Hushed and timorous, you approached.

"Oh, I'm afraid," Lizbeth whimpered. Savagely you caught her arm.

"'Sh! He'll hear you," you hissed through chattering teeth. A cloud hid the sun, and the ominous shadow fell upon you as you crouched, trembling, on the edge of the raspberry wood.

Our Yard

"'Sh!" you said. Under cover of the forest shade you crept with bated breath, on all-fours, stealthily. Oh, what was that? That awful sound, that hideous groan? From the barn it came, with a crunching of teeth and a rattle of chain. Lizbeth gave a little cry, seized you, and hid her face against your coat.

"'Sh!" you said. "That's him! Hear him!"

Through wood and prairie rang a piercing cry—

"Mother! I want my mother!"

And Lizbeth fled, wailing, across the plain. You followed—to cheer her.

"Cowardy Calf!" you said, but you did not say it till you had reached the kitchen door. And in hunting the Wild Man you never got farther than his groan.

Mornings in Our Yard the clover prairie sparkled with a million gems. The fairies

In the Morning Glow

had dropped them, dancing in the moonbeams, while you slept. Strung on a blade of grass you found a necklace of diamonds left by the queen herself in her flight at dawn, but when you plucked it, the quivering brilliants melted into water drops and trickled down your hand. Then the warm sun came and took the diamonds back to the fairies again—but your shoes were still damp with dew. And by-and-by you would be sneezing, and Mother would be taking down bottles for you, for the things that fairies wear are not good for little boys. And if ever you squash the fairies' diamonds beneath your feet, and don't change your shoes, the fairies will be angry with you, and you will be catching cold; and if you take the queen's necklace—oh, then watch out, for they will be putting a necklace of red flannel on you!

Our Yard

Wide-awake was Our Yard in the morning with its birds and wind and sunshine and your play, but when noonday dinner was over there was a yawning in the trees. The birds hushed their songs. Grandfather dozed in his chair on the porch. The green grass dozed in the sun. And as the shadows lengthened even the perils slept—Indians on the clover prairie, bear in the rhubarb thicket, Wild Man in the barn. In the apple-tree shade you lay wondering, looking up at the sky—wondering why bees purred like pussy-cats, why the sparrows bowed to you as they eyed you sidewise, what they twittered in the leaves, where the clouds went when they sailed to the end of the sky. Three clouds there were, floating above the apple-tree, and two were big and one was little.

"The big clouds are the Mother and

In the Morning Glow

Father clouds," you told yourself, for no one was there to hear, "and the little one is the Little Boy cloud, and they are out walking in the sky. And now the Mother cloud is talking to the Little Boy cloud. 'Hurry up,' she says; 'why do you walk so slow?' And the Little Boy cloud says, 'I can't go any faster 'cause my legs are so short.' And then the Father cloud laughs and says, 'Let's have some ice-cream soda.' Then the Little Boy cloud says, 'I'll take vaniller, and make it sweet,' and they all drink. And by-and-by they all go home and have supper, and after supper the Mother cloud undresses the Little Boy cloud, and puts on his nighty, and he kneels down and says, 'Now I lay me down to sleep.' And then the Mother cloud kisses the Little Boy cloud on both cheeks and on his eyes and on his curls and on his mouth twice, and

Our Yard

he cuddles down under the moon and goes to sleep. And that's all."

Far beyond the apple-tree, far beyond your ken, the three clouds floated—Father and Mother and Little Son — else your story had been longer; and in the floating of little clouds, in the making of little stories, in the sleeping of little boys, it was always easiest when Our Yard slumbered in the afternoon.

When supper was over a bonfire blazed in the western sky, just over the back fence. The clouds built it, you explained to Lizbeth, to keep themselves warm at night. It was a beautiful fire, all gold and red, but as Our Yard darkened, the fire sank lower till only the sparks remained, and sometimes the clouds came and put the sparks out too. When the moon shone you could see, through the window by your bed, the clover prairie

In the Morning Glow

and the trellis mountains, silver with fairies, and you longed to hold one in your hand. But when the night fell moonless and starless, the fairies in Our Yard groped their way — you could see their lanterns twinkling in the trees — and there were goblins under every bush, and, crouching in the black shadows, was the Wild Man, gnawing a little boy's bone. Oh, Our Yard was awful on a dark night, and when you were tucked in bed and the lamp was out and Mother away downstairs, you could hear the Wild Man crunching his bone beneath your window, and you pulled the covers over your head. But always, when you woke, Our Yard was bright and green again, for though the moon ran away some nights, the sun came every day.

With all its greenness and its brightness and its vastness and its enchanted

Our Yard

garden, Our Yard bore a heavy yoke. You were not quite sure what the burden was, but it was something about tea. Men, painted and feathered like the red Indians, had gone one night to a ship in the harbor and poured the tea into the sea. That you knew; and you had listened and heard of the midnight ride of Paul Revere.

Through the window you saw Our Yard smiling in the morning sun; trees green with summer; flight of white clouds in the sky; flight of brown birds in the bush. Wondering, you saw it there, a fair land manacled by a tyrant's hand, and the blood mounted to your cheeks.

"Mother, I want my sword."

"It is where you left it, my boy."

"And my soldier-hat and drum."

"They are under the stairs."

Over your shoulder you slung your drum. With her own hands Mother belt-

In the Morning Glow

ed your sword around you and set your cocked hat on your curls. Then twice she kissed you, and you marched away to the music of your drum. She watched you from the open door.

It was a windy morning, and you were bravest in the wind. From the back fence to the front gate, from the beehives to the red geraniums, there was a scent and stir of battle in the air. Rhubarb thicket and raspberry wood re-echoed with the beat of drums and the tramp of marching feet. Far away beyond the wood-pile hills, behind the trellis mountains where the morning-glories clung, tremulous, in the gale, even the enchanted garden woke from slumber and the flowers shuddered in their peaceful beds. On you marched, through the wind and the morning, on through Middlesex, village and farm, till you heard the cannon and the battle-cries.

Our Yard

"Halt!"

You unslung your drum. Mounting your charger, you galloped down the line.

"Forward!"

And you rode across the blood-stained clover. Into the battle you led them, sword in hand—into the thickest of the fight—while all about you, thundering in the apple-boughs, reverberating in the wood-pile hills, roared the guns of the west wind. Fair in the face of that cannonade you flung the flower of your army. Around you lay the wounded, the dead, the dying. Beneath you your charger fell, blood gushing from his torn side. A thrust bayonet swept off your cocked hat. You were down yourself. Tut! 'Twas a mere scratch—and you struggled on. Repulsed, you rallied and charged again . . . again . . . again, across the clover, to the mouths of the smoking guns.

In the Morning Glow

Afoot, covered with blood, your shattered sword gleaming in the morning sun, you stood at last on the scorched heights. Before your flashing eyes, a rout of redcoats in retreat; behind your tossing curls, the buff and blue.

A cry of triumph came down the beaten wind:

"Mother! Mother! We licked 'em!"
"Whom?"
"The Briddish!"
And Our Yard was free.

The Toy Grenadier

The Toy Grenadier

IT was a misnomer. He was not a captain at all, nor was he of the Horse Marines. He was a mere private in the Grenadier Guards, with his musket at a carry and his heels together, and his little fingers touching the seams of his pantaloons. Still, Captain Jinks was the name he went by when he first came to Our House, years ago, and Captain Jinks he will be always in your memory—the only original Captain Jinks, the ballad to the contrary notwithstanding.

It was Christmas Eve when you first

In the Morning Glow

saw him. He was stationed on sentry duty beneath a fir-tree, guarding a pile of commissary stores. He looked neither to the left nor to the right, but straight before him, and not a tremor or blink or sigh disturbed his military bearing. His bearskin was glossy as a pussy-cat's fur; his scarlet coat, with the cross of honor on his heart, fitted him like a glove, and every gilt button of it shone in the candle-light; and oh, the loveliness, the spotless loveliness, of his sky-blue pantaloons!

"My boy," said Father, "allow me to present Captain Jinks. Captain Jinks, my son."

"Oh!" you cried, the moment you clapped eyes on him. "Oh, Father! What a beautiful soldier!"

And at your praise the Captain's cheeks were scarlet. He would have saluted, no

The Toy Grenadier

doubt, had you been a military man, but you were only a civilian then.

"Take him," said Father, "and give him some rations. He's about starved, I guess, guarding those chocolates."

So you relieved the Captain of his stern vigil — or, rather, the Captain and his gun, for he refused to lay down his arms even for mess call, without orders from the officer of the guard, though he did desert his post, which was inconsistent from a military point of view, and deserved court-martial. And while he was gone the commissary stores were plundered by ruthless, sticky hands.

Lizbeth brought a new wax doll to mess with the Captain. A beautiful blonde she was, and the Captain was gallantry itself, but she was a little stiff with him, in her silks and laces, preferring, no doubt, a messmate with epaulets and sword. So

In the Morning Glow

the chat lagged till the Rag Doll came —an unassuming brunette creature—and the Captain got on very well with her. Indeed, when the Wax Doll flounced away, the Captain leaned and whispered in the Rag Doll's ear. What he said you did not hear, but the Rag Doll drew away, shyly—

"Very sudden," she seemed to say. But the Captain leaned nearer, at an angle perilous to both, and—kissed her! The Rag Doll fainted to the floor. The Captain was at his wits' end. Without orders he could not lay aside his gun, for he was a sentry, albeit off his post. Yet here was a lady in distress. The gun or the lady? The lady or the gun? The Captain struggled betwixt his honor and his love. In the very stress of his contending emotions he tottered, and would have fallen to the Rag Doll's side, but you caught

The Toy Grenadier

him just in time. Lizbeth applied the smelling-bottle to the Rag Doll's nose, and she revived. Pale, but every inch a rag lady, she rose, leaning on Lizbeth. She gave the Captain a withering glance, and swept towards the open door. The Captain did not flinch. Proudly he drew himself to his full height; his heels clicked together; his gun fell smartly to his side; and as the lady passed he looked her squarely in her scornful eyes, and bore their *congé* like a soldier.

Next morning — Christmas morning — in the trenches before the Coal Scuttle, the Captain fought with reckless bravery. The earthworks of building-blocks reached barely to his cartridge-belt, yet he stood erect in a hail of marble balls.

"Jinks, you're clean daft," cried Grandfather. "Lie down, man!"

But the Captain would not budge. Com-

In the Morning Glow

mies and glassies crashed around him. They ploughed up the earthworks before him; they did great execution on the legs of chairs and tables and other non-combatants behind. Yet there he stood, unmoved in the midst of the carnage, his heels together, his little fingers just touching the seams of his pantaloons. It was for all the world as though he were on dress parade. Perhaps he was—for while he stood there, valorous in that Christmas fight, his eyes were on the heights of Rocking Chair beyond, where, safe from the marble hail, sat the Rag Doll with Lizbeth and the waxen blonde.

There was a rumble—a crash through the torn earthworks—a shock—a scream from the distant heights—and the Captain fell. A monstrous glassy had struck him fairly in the legs, and owing to his military habit of standing with them

The Toy Grenadier

close together—well, it was all too sad, too harrowing, to relate. An ambulance corps of Grandfather and Uncle Ned carried the crippled soldier to the Tool Chest Hospital. He was just conscious, that was all. The operation he bore with great fortitude, refusing to take chloroform, and insisting on dying with his musket beside him, if die he must. What seemed to give him greatest anguish was his heels, for, separated at last, they would not click together now; and his little fingers groped nervously for the misplaced seams of his pantaloons.

Long afterwards, when the Captain had left his cot for active duty again, it was recalled that the very moment when he fell so gallantly in the trenches that day a lady was found unconscious, flat on her face, at the foot of Rocking Chair Hill.

Captain Jinks was never the same after

In the Morning Glow

that. Still holding his gun as smartly as before, there was, on the other hand, a certain carelessness of attire, a certain dulness of gilt buttons, a smudginess of scarlet coat, as though it were thumb-marked; and dark clouds were beginning to lower in the clear azure of his pantaloons. There was, withal, a certain rakishness of bearing not provided for in the regulations; a little uncertainty as to legs; a tilt and limp, as it were, in sharp contrast to the trim soldier who had guarded the commissary chocolates under the Christmas fir. Moreover—though his comrades at arms forbore to mention it, loving him for his gallant service—he was found one night, flat on his face, under the dinner-table. Now the Captain had always been abstemious before. Liquor of any kind he had shunned as poison, holding that it spotted his uniform; and once when forced

The Toy Grenadier

to drink from Lizbeth's silver cup, at the end of a dusty march, his lips paled at the contaminating touch, his red cheeks blanched, and his black mustache, in a single drink, turned gray. But here he lay beneath the festive board, bedraggled, his nose buried in the soft rug, hopelessly inarticulate—though the last symptom was least to be wondered at, since he had always been a silent man.

You shook him where he lay. There was no response. You dragged him forth in his shame and set him on his feet again, but he staggered and fell. Yet as he lay there in his cups—oh, mystery of discipline!—his heels were close together, his toes turned out, his musket was at a carry, and his little fingers were just touching the seams of his pantaloons.

For the good of the service Mother offered to retire the Captain on half pay,

In the Morning Glow

and give him free lodging on the garret stair, but he scorned the proposal, and you backed him in his stand. All his life he had been a soldier. Now, with war and rumors of war rife in the land, should he, Captain Jinks, a private in the Grenadier Guards, lay down his arms for the piping peace of a garret stair? No, by gad, sir! No! And he stayed; and, strangest thing of all, he was yet to fight and stand guard and suffer as he had never done before.

But while the Captain thus sadly went down hill, the Rag Doll retired to a modest villa in the closet country up-stairs. It was quiet there, and she could rest her shattered nerves. Whether she blamed herself for her rejected lover's downfall, or whether it was mere petulance at the social triumphs of the waxen blonde, is a question open to debate. Sentimentalists

The Toy Grenadier

will find the former theory more to their fancy, but the blonde and her friends told a different tale. Be that as it may, the Rag Doll went away.

January passed in barracks; then February and March, with only an occasional scouting after cattle-thieves and brigand bands. The Captain chafed at such inactivity.

"War! You call this war!" his very bristling manner seemed to say. "By gad! sir, when I was in the trenches before . . . "

It was fine then to see the Captain and Grandfather—both grizzled veterans with tales to tell—side by side before the library fire. When Grandfather told the story of Johnny Reb in the tall grass, the Captain was visibly moved.

"Jinks," Grandfather would say— "Jinks, you know how it is yourself—

In the Morning Glow

when the bacon's wormy and the coffee's thin, and there's a man with a gun before you and a girl with a tear behind."

And at the mention of the girl and the tear the Captain would turn away.

Spring came, and with it the marching orders for which you and the Captain had yearned so long. There was a stir in the barracks that morning. The Captain was drunk again, it is true, but drunk this time with joy. He could not march in the ranks—he was too far gone for that—so you stationed him on a wagon to guard the commissary stores.

A blast from the bugle — Assembly — and you fell into line.

"Forward—*March!*"

And you marched away, your drum beating a double-quick, the Captain swaying ignominiously on the wagon and hugging his old brown gun. As the

The Toy Grenadier

Guards swung by the reviewing-stand, their arms flashing in the sun, the Captain did not raise his eyes. So he never knew that looking down upon his shame that April day sat his rag lady, with Lizbeth and the waxen blonde. Her cheeks were pale, but her eyes were tearless. She did not utter a sound as her tottering lover passed. She just leaned far out over the flag-hung balcony and watched him as he rode away.

It was a hard campaign. Clover Plain, Wood-pile Mountain, and the Raspberry Wilderness are names to conjure with. From the back fence to the front gate, from the beehives to the red geraniums, the whole land ran with blood. Brevetted for personal gallantry on the Wood-pile Heights, you laid aside your drum for epaulets and sword. The Guards and the Captain drifted from your ken. When

In the Morning Glow

you last saw him he was valiantly defending a tulip pass, and defying a regiment of the Black Ant Brigade to come and take him—by gad! sirs—if they dared.

The war went on. Days grew into weeks, weeks into months, and the summer passed. Search in camps and battle-fields revealed no trace of Captain Jinks. Sitting by the camp-fire on blustering nights, your thoughts went back to the old comrade of the winter days.

"Poor Captain Jinks!" you sighed.

"Jinks?" asked Grandfather, laying down his book.

"Yes. He's lost. Didn't you know?"

"Jinks among the missing!" Grandfather cried. Then he gazed silently into the fire.

"Poor old Jinks!" he mused. "He was a brave soldier, Jinks was—a brave soldier, sir." He puffed reflectively on his

The Toy Grenadier

corn-cob pipe. Presently he spoke again, more sadly than before:

"But he had one fault, Jinks had—just one, sir. He was a leetle too fond o' his bottle on blowy nights."

November came. The year and the war were drawing to a close. Before Grape Vine Ridge the enemy lay intrenched for a final desperate stand. To your council of war in the fallen leaves came Grandfather, a scarf around his throat, its loose ends flapping in the gale. He leaned on his cane; you, on your sword.

"Bring up your guns, boy," he cried. "Bring up your heavy guns. Fling your cavalry to the left, your infantry to the right. 'Up, Guards, and at 'em!' Cold steel, my boy—as Jinks used to say."

Grandfathers for counsel; little boys for war. At five that night the enemy surrendered—horse, foot, and a hundred

In the Morning Glow

guns. Declining the General's proffered sword, you rode back across the battle-field to your camp in the fallen leaves. The afternoon was waning. In the gathering twilight your horse stumbled on a prostrate form. You dismounted, knelt, brushed back the leaves, peered into the dimmed eyes and ashen face.

"'Captain!" you cried. "Captain Jinks!" And at your call came Lizbeth, running, dragging the Rag Doll by her hand. Breathless they knelt beside him where he lay.

"Oh, it's Captain Jinks," said Lizbeth, but softly, when she saw. Prone on the battle-field lay the wounded Grenadier, his uniform gray with service in the wind and rain.

"Captain!" you cried again, but he did not hear you. Then the Rag Doll bent her face to his, in the twilight, though she

The Toy Grenadier

could not speak. A glimmer of recognition blazed for a moment, but faded in the Captain's eyes.

"He's tired marching, I guess," said Lizbeth.

"'Sh!" you said. "He's dying."

You bent lower to feel his fluttering pulse. You placed your ear to the cross of honor, rusted, on his breast. His heart was silent. And so he died—on the battlefield, his musket at his side, his heels together, his little fingers just touching the seams of his pantaloons.

Father

Father

EVERY evening at half-past six there was a sound of footsteps on the front porch. You ran, you and Lizbeth, and by the time you had reached the door it opened suddenly from without, and you each had a leg of Father. Mother was just behind you in the race, and though she did not shout or dance, or pull his coat or seize his bundles, she won his first kiss, so that you and Lizbeth came in second after all.

"Hello, Buster!" he would sing out to you, so that you cried, "My name ain't

In the Morning Glow

Buster—it's Harry," at which he would be mightily surprised. But he always called Lizbeth by her right name.

"Well, Lizbeth," he would say, kneeling, for you had pulled him down to you, bundles and all, and Lizbeth would cuddle down into his arms and say:

"*Fa*-ther."

"What?"

"Why, Father, now what do you think? My Sally doll has got the measles awful."

"No! You don't say?"

And "Father!" you would yell into his other ear, for while Lizbeth used one, you always used the other—using one by two persons at the same time being strictly forbidden.

"Father."

"Yes, my son.

"The Jones boy was here to-day and —and—and he said—why, now, he said—"

Father

"*Fa*-ther" (it was Lizbeth talking into *her* ear now), "do you think my Sally doll—"

It was Mother who rescued Father and his bundles at last and carried you off to supper, and when your mouth was not too full you finished telling him what the Jones boy said, and he listened gravely, and prescribed for the Sally doll. Though he came home like that every night except Sunday in all the year, you always had something new to tell him in both ears, and it was always, to all appearances, the most wonderful thing he had ever heard.

But now and then there were times when you did not yearn for the sound of Father's footsteps on the porch.

"Wait till Father comes home and Mother tells him what a bad, bad boy you have been!"

"I don't care," you whispered, defiantly,

In the Morning Glow

all to yourself, scowling out of the window, but "Tick-tock, tick-tock" went the clock on the mantel-shelf — "Tick-tock, tick-tock"—more loudly, more swiftly than you had ever heard it tick before. Still you were brave in the broad light of day, and if sun and breeze and bird-songs but held out long enough, Mother might forget. You flattened your nose against the pane. There was a dicky-bird hopping on the apple-boughs outside. You heard him twittering. If you were only a bird, now, instead of a little boy. Birds were so happy and free. Nobody ever made them stay in-doors on an afternoon made for play. If only a fairy godmother would come in a gold coach and turn you into a bird. Then you would fly away, miles and miles, and when they looked for you, at half-past six, you would be chirping in some cherry-tree.

Father

"Tick-tock, tick-tock — whir-r-r! One! Two! Three! Four! Five!" struck the clock on the mantel-shelf. The bright day was running away from you, leaving you far behind to be caught, at half-past six — caught and . . .

But Father might not come home to supper to-night! Once he did not. At the thought the sun lay warm upon your cheek, and you rapped on the pane bravely at the dicky-bird outside. The bird flew away.

"Tick-tock, tick-tock, tick-tock, tick-tock."

Swiftly the day passed. Terribly fell the black night, fastening its shadows on you and all the world. Grimly Mother passed you, without a look or word. She pulled down the window shades. One by one she lighted the lamps—the tall piano-lamp with the red globe, the little

In the Morning Glow

green lamp on the library-table, the hanging lamp in the dining-room. Already the supper-table was set.

The clock struck six!

You watched Mother out of the corners of your eyes. Had she forgotten?

"Mother," you said, engagingly. "See me stand on one leg."

"Mother does not care to look at naughty little boys."

"Tick-tock, tick-tock, tick-tock, tick-tock."

You were very little to punish. Besides, you were not feeling very well. It was not your tummy, nor your head, nor yet the pussy-scratch on your finger. It was a deeper pain.

"Tick-tock, tick-tock."

If you should die like the Jones boy's little brother and be put in the cemetery on the hill, they would be sorry.

Father

"Tick-tock, tick-tock."

Mother went to the window and peered out.

"TICK-TOCK!"

"Whir-r-r—"

And the clock struck half-past six!

Steps sounded upon the porch—Mother was going to the door—it opened!

"Where's Buster?"

And Mother told!

... And somehow when Father spanked it always seemed as if he were meddling. He was an outsider all day. Why, then, did he concern himself so mightily at night?

After supper Father would sit before the fire with you on one knee and Lizbeth on the other, while Mother sewed, till by-and-by, just when you were most comfy and the talk most charming, he would say:

"Well, Father must go now."

In the Morning Glow

"Oh no, Father. Don't go yet."

"But Father must. He must go to Council-meeting."

"What's a Council-meeting, Father?" you asked, and while he was telling you he would be putting on his coat.

"Don't sit up for me," he would tell Mother, and the door would shut at half-past seven just as it had opened at half-past six, with the same sound of footsteps on the porch.

"Oh, dear," you would say. "Father's always going somewhere. I guess he doesn't like to stay home, Mother."

Then Mother would take you and Lizbeth on her lap.

"Dearies, Father would love to stay at home and play with you and Mother, but he can't. All day long he has to work to take care of us and buy us bread-and-butter—"

Father

"And chocolate cake, Mother?"

"Yes, and chocolate cake. And he goes to the Council to help the other men take care of Ourtown so that the burglars won't get in or the street-lamps go out and leave us in the dark."

Your eyes were very round. That night after you and Lizbeth were in bed and the lights were out, you thought of the Council and the burglars so that you could not sleep, and while you lay there thinking, the wolf-wind began to howl outside. Then suddenly you heard the patter, patter, patter of its feet upon the roof. You shuddered and drew the bedclothes over your head. What if It got inside? Could It bite through the coverlet with its sharp teeth? Would the Council come and save you just in time? . . . Which would be worse, a wolf or a burglar? A wolf, of course, for a burglar might have a little

In the Morning Glow

boy of his own somewhere, in bed, curled up and shivering, with the covers over his head. . . . But what if the burglar had no little boy? Did burglars *ever* have little boys? . . . How could a man ever be brave enough to be a burglar, in the dead of night, crawling through windows into pitch-dark rooms, . . . into little boys' rooms, . . . crawling in stealthily with pistols and false-faces and l-lanterns? . . .

But That One was crawling in! Right into your room, . . . right in over the window-sill, . . . like a cat, . . . with a false-face on, and pistols, loaded and pointed right at you. . . . You tried to call; . . . your voice was dried up in your throat, . . . and all the time He was coming nearer, . . . nearer, . . . nearer . . .

"Bad dream, was it, little chap?" asked the Council, holding you close to his coat, all smoky of cigars, and patting your cheek.

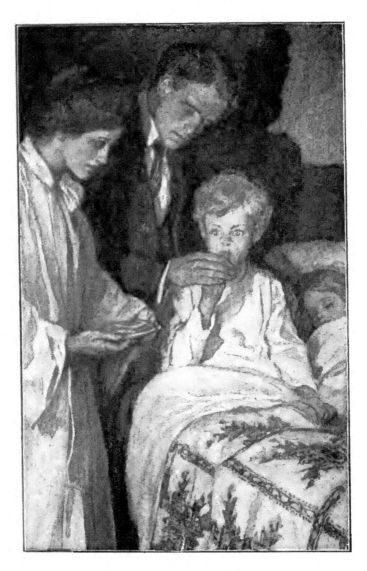
"'BAD DREAM, WAS IT, LITTLE CHAP?'"

Father

"F-father, where did he go?"

"Who go, my boy?"

"Why, the burglar, Father."

"There wasn't any burglar, child."

"Why, *yes*, Father. I saw him. Right there. Coming through the window."

And it took Father and Mother and two oatmeal crackers and a drink of water to convince you that it was all a dream. So whether it was in frightening burglars away, or keeping the street-lamps burning, or smoking cigars, or soothing a little boy with a nightmare and a fevered head, the Council was a useful body, and always came just in time.

On week-day mornings Father had gone to work when you came down-stairs, but on Sunday mornings, when you awoke, a trifle earlier if anything—

"Father!"

Silence.

In the Morning Glow

"Father!" a little louder.

Then a sleepy "Yes."

"We want to get up."

"It isn't time yet. You children go to sleep."

You waited. Then—

"Father, is it time yet?"

"No. You children lie still."

So you and Lizbeth, wide-awake, whispered together; and then, to while away the time while Father slept, you played Indian, which required two little yells from you to begin with (when the Indian You arrived in your war-paint) and two big yells from Lizbeth to end with (when the Paleface She was being scalped).

Then Father said it was "no use," and Mother took a hand. You were quiet after that, but it was yawny lying there with the sun so high. You listened. Not a sound came from Father and Mother's

Father

room. You rose cautiously, you and Lizbeth, in your little bare feet. You stole softly across the floor. The door was a crack open, so you peeked in, your face even with the knob and Lizbeth's just below. And then, at one and the same instant, you both said "Boo!" and grinned; and the harder you grinned the harder Father tried not to laugh, which was a sign that you could scramble into bed with him, you on one side and Lizbeth on the other, cuddling down close while Mother went to see about breakfast.

It was very strange, but while it had been so hard to drowse in your own bed, the moment you were in Father's you did not want to get up at all. Indeed, it was Father who wanted to get up first, and it was you who cried that it was not time.

Week-days were always best for most

In the Morning Glow

things, but for two reasons Sunday was the best day of all. One reason was Sunday dinner. The other was Father. On Sunday the dinner-table was always whitest with clean linen and brightest with silver and blue china and fullest of good things to eat, and sometimes Company came and brought their children with them. On Sunday, too, there was no store to keep, and Father could stay at home all day.

He came down to breakfast in slippers and a beautiful, wide jacket, which was brown to match the coffee he always took three cups of, and the cigar which he smoked afterwards in a big chair with his feet thrust out on a little one. While he smoked he would read the paper, and sometimes he would laugh and read it out loud to Mother; and sometimes he would say, "That's so," and lay down his paper and talk to Mother like the minister's sermon. And once

Father

he talked so loudly that he said "Damn." Mother looked at you, for you were listening, and sent you for her work-basket up-stairs. After that, when you talked loudest to Lizbeth or the Jones boy, you said "Damn," too, like Father, till Mother overheard you and explained that only fathers and grandfathers and bad little boys ever said such things. It wasn't a pretty word, she said, for nice little boys like you.

"But, Mother, if the bad little boys say it, why do the good fathers say it—hm?"

Mother explained that, too. Little boys should mind their mothers, she said.

It was easy enough not to say the word when you talked softly, but when you talked loudest it was hard to remember what Mother said. For when you talked softly, somehow, you always remembered Mother, and when you talked loudly it was Father you remembered best.

In the Morning Glow

The sun rose high and warm. It was a long time after breakfast. Fragrance came from the kitchen to where you sat in the library, all dressed-up, looking at picture-books and waiting for dinner, and wondering if there would be pie. Father was all dressed-up, too, and while he read silently, you and Lizbeth felt his cheeks softly with your finger-tips. Where the prickers had been at breakfast-time it was as smooth as velvet now. Father's collar was as white as snow. In place of his jacket he wore his long, black Sunday coat, and in his shoes you could almost see your face.

"Father's beautifulest on Sunday," Lizbeth said.

"So am I," you said, proudly, looking down your blouse and trousers to the shine of your Sunday shoes.

"So are you, too," you added kindly to Lizbeth, who was all in white and curls.

Father

Then you drew a little chair beside Father's and sat, quiet and very straight, with your legs crossed carelessly like his and an open book like his in your lap. And when Father changed his legs, you changed your legs, too. Lizbeth looked at you two awhile awesomely. Then she brought her little red chair and sat beside you with the Aladdin book on her lap, but she did not cross her legs. And so you sat there, all three, clean and dressed-up and beautiful, by the bay-window, while the sun lay warm and golden on the library rug, and sweeter and sweeter grew the kitchen smells.

Then dinner came, and the last of it was best because it was sweetest, and if Company were not there you cried:

"It's going to be pie to-day, isn't it, Mother?"

But Mother would only smile mysterious-

In the Morning Glow

ly while the roast was carried away. Then Lizbeth guessed.

"It's pudding," she said.

"No, pie," you cried again, "'cause yesterday was pudding."

"Now, Father, you guess," said Lizbeth.

"I guess?"

"Yes, Father."

And at that Father would knit his brows and put one finger to one side of his nose, so that he could think the harder, and by-and-by he would say:

"I know. I'll bet it's custard."

"Oh *no*, Father," you broke in, for you liked pie best, and even to admit the possibility of custard, aloud, might make it come true.

"Then it's lemon jelly with cream," said Father, trying another finger to his nose and pondering deeply.

"Oh, you only have one guess," cried

Father

you and Lizbeth together, and Father, cornered, stuck to the jelly and cream.

"Oh, dear," Lizbeth said, "I don't see what good it does to brush off the crumbs in the middle of dinner."

Silence fell upon the table, you and Lizbeth holding Father's outstretched hands. Your eyes were wide, the better to see. Your lips were parted, the better, doubtless, to hear. Only Mother was serene, for only Mother knew. And then through the stillness came the sound of rattling plates.

"Pie," you whispered.

"Pudding," whispered Lizbeth.

"Jelly," whispered Father, hoarsely.

The door swung open. You rose in your seats, you and Lizbeth and Father, craning your necks to see, and, seeing—

"*Pie!*" you cried, triumphantly.

"Ah!" said Father, lifting his pie-crust gayly with the tip of his fork.

In the Morning Glow

"Apples," you said, peeping under your crust.

"Apples, my son? Apples? Why, no. Bless my soul! As I live, this is a robber's cave filled with sacks of gold."

"Oh, *Father!*" you cried, incredulous, not knowing how to take him yet; but you peeped again, and under your pie-crust it *was* like a cave, and the little slices of juicy apple lay there like sacks of gold.

"And see!" said Father, pointing with his fork, "there is the entrance to the cave, and when the policemen chased the robbers—pop! they went, right into their hole, like rabbits."

And sure enough, in the upper crusts were the little cuts through which the robbers popped. Your eyes widened.

"And oh, Father," you said, "the smoke can come out through the little holes when the robbers build their fire."

Father

"Aha!" cried Father, fiercely. "I'm the policeman breaking into the cave while the robbers are away," and he took a bite.

"And I'm another policeman," you cried, catching the spirit of the thing and taking a bigger bite than Father's.

"And I'm a policeman's wife coming along, too," said Lizbeth, helping herself, so that Mother said:

"John, John, how am I ever going to teach these children table manners when—"

"But see, Mother, see!" Father explained, taking another bite, and ignoring Mother's eyes. "If we don't get the gold away the robbers will come back and—"

"Kill us!" you broke in.

"Yes, kill us, Mother!" shouted Father, balancing another sack of gold on the end of his fork. "Yes, yes, Mother, don't you see?"

"I see," said Mother, just between laugh

In the Morning Glow

and frown, and when the robbers came back around the coffee-pot hill, lo! there was no gold or cave awaiting them—only three plates scraped clean, and two jubilant policemen and a policeman's wife, full of gold.

And when Father was Father again, leaning on the back of Mother's chair, she said to him, "You're nothing but a great big boy," so that Father chuckled, his cheek against hers and his eyes shining. That was the way with Father. Six days he found quite long enough to be a man; so on Sunday he became a boy.

The gate clicked behind you, Father in the middle and you and Lizbeth holding each a hand, and keeping step with him when you could, running a little now and then to catch up again. Your steps were always longest on Sunday when you walked with Father, and even Lizbeth

Father

knew you then for a little man, and peeked around Father's legs to see you as you strode along. Father was proud of you, too, though he did not tell you. He just told other people when he thought you could not hear.

"Little pitchers have big ears," Mother would warn him then, but you heard quite plainly out of one ear, and it was small at that.

Everybody looked as you three went down the shady street together, and the nice young ladies gave you smiles and the nice old ladies gave you flowers, handing them out to you over their garden walls.

"Thank you. My name is Harry," you said.

"And I'm Lizbeth," said little sister. And as you passed on your stride grew longer and your voice sank bigger and deeper in your throat, like Father's.

In the Morning Glow

But it wasn't the town you liked best to walk in with Father in the long, warm Sunday afternoons. It was the river-side, where the willows drooped over the running waters, and the grass was deepest and greenest and waved in the sun. On the meadow-bank at the water's silver edge you sat down together.

"Who can hear the most?" asked Father.

You listened.

"I hear the river running over the log," you said, softly.

"And the birds," whispered Lizbeth.

"And the wind in the willows," said Father.

"And the cow-bells tinkling way, way off," you added, breathlessly.

"Oh, and I hear the grass whispering," said Lizbeth.

"And oh, a bee," you cried.

"And something else," said Father.

"'FATHER, WHAT DO YOU THINK WHEN YOU DON'T SAY ANYTHING, BUT JUST LOOK?'"

Father

You held your breath and listened. From the distant village the wind blew you faintly the sound of—

"Church-bells," cried you and Lizbeth together.

You fell to playing in the long grass. Lizbeth gathered daisies for Mother. You lay with your face just over the river-bank, humming a little song and gazing down into the mirror of the waters. You wondered how it would feel to be a little boy-fish, darting in and out among the river grasses.

By-and-by you went back to Father and sat beside him with your cheek against his arm.

"Father."

"Yes."

"What do you think when you don't say anything, but just look?"

"When I just look?"

In the Morning Glow

"Yes. Do you think what I do?"

"Well, what do you think?"

"Why, I think I'd like to be a big man like you and wear a long coat, and take my little boy and girl out walking. Did you think that, Father?"

"No. I was thinking how nice it would be just to be a little boy again like you and go out walking by the river with my father."

"Oh, Father, how funny! I wanted to be you and you wanted to be me. I guess people always want to be somebody else when they just look and don't say anything."

"What makes you think that, my boy?"

"Well, there's Grandmother. *She* sits by the window all day long and just looks and looks, and wishes she was an angel with Grandfather up in the sky."

"And Lizbeth?"

Father

"Oh, Lizbeth wishes she was Mother."

"And how about Mother? Does she wish she were somebody else, do you think?"

"Oh no, Father, *she* doesn't, 'cause then she wouldn't have me and Lizbeth. Besides, she don't have time to just sit and look, Mother don't."

Your eyes were big and shining. Father just looked and looked a long time.

"And what do you think *now*, Father?"

"I was thinking of Mother waiting for you and Lizbeth and Father, and wondering why we don't come home."

And almost always after that, when you went out walking with Father, Sundays, Mother went with you. It seemed strange at first, but fine, to have her sit with you on the river-bank and just look and look and look, smiling but never saying a word; and though you asked her

In the Morning Glow

many times what she thought about as she sat there dreaming, she was never once caught wishing that she were anybody but her own self. She was happy, she told you; but while it was you she told, she would be looking at Father.

Oh, it was golden in the morning glow, when you were a little boy. But clouds skurried across the sky—black clouds, storm clouds—casting their chill and shadow for a while over all Our Yard, darkening Our House, so that a little boy playing on the hearth-rug left his toy soldier prostrate there to wander, wondering, from room to room.

"Mother, why doesn't Father play with us like he used to?"

"Mother, why do you sew and sew and sew all the time? Hm, Mother?"

All through the long evenings till bed-time came, and long afterwards, Father

Father

and Mother talked low together before the fire. The murmur of their voices downstairs was the last thing you heard before you fell asleep. It sounded like the brook in the meadow where the little green frogs lived, hopping through water-rings.

Of those secret conferences by the fire you could make nothing at all. Mother stopped you whenever you drew near.

"Run away, dear, and play."

You frowned and sidled off as far as the door, lingering wistfully.

"Father, the Jones boy made fun of me to-day. He called me Patchy-pants."

"Never mind what the Jones boy says," Mother broke in; but Father said, "He ought to have a new pair, Mother." You brightened at that.

"The Jones boy's got awful nice pants," you said; "all striped like a zebra."

Father smiled a little at that. Mother

In the Morning Glow

looked down at her sewing, saying never a word. That night you dreamed you had new pants, all spotted like a leopard, and you were proud, for every one knows that a leopard could whip a zebra, once he jumped upon his back.

Leaning on the garden fence, the Jones boy watched you as you sprinkled the geraniums with your little green watering-can.

"Where'd you get it?" he asked.

"Down at my father's store," you replied, loftily, for the Jones boy had no watering-can.

"Your father hasn't got a store any more."

"He has, too," you replied.

"He hasn't, either, 'cause my pa says he hasn't."

"I don't care what your pa says. My father has, too, got a store."

"He hasn't."

Father

"He has."

"He hasn't, either."

"He has, teether."

"I say he hasn't."

"And I say he has," you screamed, and threw the watering-can straight at the Jones boy. It struck the fence and the water splashed all over him so that he retreated to the road. There in a rage he hurled stones at you.

"Your — father — hasn't — got — any — store — any — more — old — Patchy-pants — old—Patchy-pants—old—"

And then suddenly the Jones boy fled, and when you looked around there was Father standing behind you by the geraniums.

"Never mind what the Jones boy says," he told you, and he was not angry with you for throwing the watering-can. The little green spout of it was broken when

In the Morning Glow

you picked it up, but Father said he would buy you a new one.

"To-morrow, Father?"

"No, not to-morrow—some day."

You and Lizbeth, tumbling down-stairs to breakfast, found Father sitting before the fire.

"Father!" you cried, astonished, for it was not Sunday, and though you ran to him he did not hear you till you pounced upon him in his chair.

"Oh, Father," you said, joyfully, "are you going to stay home and play with us all day?"

"*Fa*-ther!" cried Lizbeth. "Will you play house with us?"

"Oh no, Father. Play *store* with us," you cried.

"Don't bother Father," Mother said, but Father just held you both in his arms and would not let you go.

Father

"No—let them stay," he said, and Mother slipped away.

"Mother's got an awful cold," said Lizbeth. "Her eyes—"

"So has Father; only Father's cold is in his voice," you said.

You scarcely waited to eat your breakfast before you were back again to Father by the fire, telling him of the beautiful games just three could play. But while you were telling him the door-bell rang, and there were two men with books under their arms, come to see Father. They stayed with him all day long—you could hear them muttering in the library—and all day you looked wistfully at the closed door, lingering there lest Father should come out to play and find you gone.

He did not come out till dinner-time. After dinner he walked in the garden alone. He held a cigar in his clinched teeth.

In the Morning Glow

"Why don't you smoke the cigar, Father?"

He did not hear you. He just walked up and down, up and down, with his eyes on the ground and his hands thrust hard into the pockets of his coat.

Mother watched him for a moment through the window. Then with her own hands she built a fire in the grate, for the night was chill. Before it she drew an easy-chair, and put Father's smoking-jacket on the back of it and set his slippers to warm against the fender. On a reading-table near by she laid the little blue china ash-tray you had given Father for Christmas, and beside it a box of matches ready for his hand. Then she called him in.

He came and sat there before the fire, saying nothing, but looking into the flames—looking, looking, till your mind ran back

Father

to a Sunday afternoon in summer by the river-side.

"I know what you are thinking, Father."

Slowly he turned his head to you, so that you knew he was listening though he did not speak.

"You're thinking how nice it would be, Father, if you were a little boy like me."

He made no answer. Mother came and sat on one of the arms of his chair, her cheek against his hair. Lizbeth undressed her dolls for the night, crooning a lullaby. One by one you dropped your marbles into their little box. Then you rose and sat like Mother on an arm of Father's chair. For a while you dreamed there, drowsy, in the glow.

"Mother," you said, softly.

"Yes," she whispered back to you.

"Mother, isn't it *fine?*" you said.

"Fine, dearie?"

In the Morning Glow

"Yes, Mother, everything . . . 'specially—"

"Yes, sweetheart?"

"—'specially just having Father."

Father gave a little jump; seized you; crushed you in his arms, stars shining in his brimming eyes.

"Little chap—little chap," he cried, but could get no further, till by-and-by—

"Mother," he said—and his voice was clear and strong—"Mother, with a little chap like that and two girls like you and Lizbeth—"

His voice caught, but he shook it free again.

"—*any* man could begin—all over again—and *win*," he said.

"'MOTHER,' YOU SAID, SOFTLY"

Mother

Mother

 you said.
"And what's that?"
"B."
"And that?"
"C."

You sat on Mother's lap. The wolf-wind howled at the door, and you shuddered, cuddling down in Mother's arms and the glow. The wilder the wolf-wind howled, the softer was the lamp-light, the redder were the apples on the table, the warmer was the fire.

On your knees lay the picture-book with its sad, sad little tale. Mother read

In the Morning Glow

it to you—she had read it fifty times before—her face grave, her voice low and tragic, while you listened with bated breath:

> "Who killed Cock Robin?
> 'I,' said the Sparrow,
> 'With my bow and arrow—
> I killed Cock Robin.'"

It was the first murder you had ever heard about. You saw it all, the hideous spectacle — a beautiful, warm, red breast pierced by that fatal dart — a poor, soft little birdie, dead, by an assassin's hand. A lump rose in your throat. A tear rose in your eye—two tears, three tears. They rolled down your cheek. They dropped, hot and sad, on the fish with his little dish, on the owl with his spade and trowel, on the rook with his little book.

"P-poor Cock R-robin!"

"There, there, dear. Don't cry."

"THE PICTURE-BOOK"

Mother

"But, M-mother—the Sparrow—he k-killed him."

Alas, yes! The Sparrow had killed him, for the book said so, but had you heard?

"N-no, w-what?"

The book, it seems, like other books, had told but half the story. Mother knew the other half. Cock Robin was murdered, murdered in cold blood, it was true, but —O merciful, death-winged arrow!—he had gone where the good birds go. And there—O joy!—he had met his robin wife and his little robin boy, who had gone before.

"And I expect they are all there now, dear," she told you, kissing your tear-stained cheek, "the happiest robins that ever were."

Dry and wide were your eyes. In the place where the good birds go, you saw Cock Robin. His eyes and his fat, red

In the Morning Glow

breast were bright again. He chirped. He sang. He hopped from bough to bough, with his robin wife and his little robin boy. For in the mending of little stories or the mending of little hearts, like the mending of little stockings, Mother was wonderful.

In those times there were knees to your stockings, knees with holes in them at the end of the day, with the soiled skin showing through.

"Just look!" Mother would cry. "Just look there! And I'd only just mended them."

"Well, you see, Mother, when you play Black Bear—"

"I see," she said, and before you went to bed you would be sitting on the edge of a tub, paddling your feet in the water.

"You dirty boy," she would be saying, scrubbing at the scratched, black knees;

"BEFORE YOU WENT TO BED"

Mother

but when you were shining again she would be saying—

"You darling!"

And though your stockings were whole in the clean of morning when you scampered out into the sun, in the dirt of night when you scampered back again—O skein, where is thy yarn? O darning-needle, where is thy victory?

Summer mornings, in the arbor-seat of the garden, Mother would be sewing, her lap brimming, her work-basket at her feet, the sun falling golden through the trellised green. In the nap of the afternoon, when even the birds drowsed and the winds slept, she would be sewing, ever sewing. And when night fell and the dishes were put away, she would be sewing still, in the lamp-light's yellow glow.

"Mother, why do you sew and sew?"

In the Morning Glow

"To make my little boy blue sailor suits and my little girl white frocks, and to stop the holes."

"Do you like to sew, Mother?"

"I don't mind it."

"But doesn't it make you tired, Mother?"

"Oh, now and then."

"But I should think you'd rest sometimes, Mother."

"Should you, dear?"

"Yes, I would. Oh, I'd sew a *little*—just enough—and then I'd play."

"But Mother does sew *just enough,* and it takes all day, my dear. What do you say to that?"

You pondered.

"Well," you said, and stopped.

"Well?" she said, and laughed. Then you laughed, too.

"A mother," you told them afterwards,

Mother

"is a person what takes care of you, and loves you, and sews and sews—just enough —all day."

Since mothers take care of little boys, they told you, little boys should take care of their mothers, too. So right in front of her you stood, bravely, your fists clinched, your lips trembling, your eyes flashing with rage and tears.

"You sha'n't touch my mother!"

But Mother's arms stole swiftly around you, pinning your own to your side.

"Father was only fooling, dear," she said, kneeling behind you and folding you to her breast. "See, he's laughing at us."

"Why, little chap," he said, "Father was only playing."

Mother wiped away your tears, smiling at them, but proudly. You looked doubtfully at Father, who held out his arms to

In the Morning Glow

you; then slowly you went to him, urged by Mother's hand.

"You must always take care of Mother like that," he said, "and never let any one hurt her, or bother her, when Father's away."

"Mother's little knight," she said, kissing your brow. And ever afterwards she was safe when you were near.

"Oh, that Mrs. Waddles. I wish she wouldn't bother me."

Under her breath Mother said it, but you heard, and you hated Mrs. Waddles with all your soul, and her day of reckoning came. Mother was in the garden and did not hear. You answered the knock yourself.

"Little darling, how—"

"You can't see my mother to-day," you said, stiffly.

"That's very strange," said Mrs. Waddles, with a forward step.

Mother

"No," you said, a little louder, throwing yourself into the breach and holding the door-knob with all your might. "No! You mustn't come in!"

"You impertinent little child!" cried Mrs. Waddles, threateningly, but you faced her down, raising your voice again:

"You can't see my mother any more," you repeated, firmly.

"And why not, I'd like to know?" demanded the old lady, swelling visibly. "Why not, I'd like to know?"

"'Cause I'm to take care of my mother when my father's away, and he said not to let anybody bother her that she don't want to see."

It was a long explanation and took all your breath.

"Oh, is *that* it?" cackled Mrs. Waddles, with withering scorn. "And how do you

In the Morning Glow

know that your mother doesn't want to see me—*hey?*"

" 'Cause—she—said—so!"

You separated your words like the A B C book, that Mrs. Waddles might understand. It was a master-stroke. Gasping, her face on fire, gathering her skirts together with hands that trembled in their black silk mitts, Mrs. Waddles turned and swept away.

"I never!" she managed to utter as she slammed the gate.

You shut the door softly, the battle won, and went back to the garden.

"Well, *that's* over," you said, with a sigh, as Mother herself would have said it.

"What's over, dear?"

"Mrs. Waddles," you replied.

So you took care of Mother so well that she loved you more and more as the days of your knighthood passed; and she took care of you so well that your cheeks grew

Mother

rosier and your eyes brighter and your legs stronger, and you loved her more and more with the days of her motherhood.

Even being sick was fine in those days, for she brought you little things in bowls with big spoons in them, and you ate till you wanted more—a sign that you would not die. And so you lay in the soft of the pillows, with the patchwork coverlet that Mother made with her own hands. There was the white silk triangle from her wedding-gown, and a blue one from a sash that was her Sunday best, long ago, when she was a little girl. There was a soft-gray piece from a dress of Grandmother's, and a bright-pink one that was once Lizbeth's, and a striped one, blue and yellow, that was once Father's necktie in the gay plumage of his youth.

As you lay there, sick and drowsy, the bridal triangle turned to snow, cold and

In the Morning Glow

white and pure, and you heard sleigh-bells and saw the Christmas cards with the little church in the corner, its steeple icy, but its windows warm and red with the Christmas glow. That was the white triangle. But the blue one, next, was sky, and when you saw it you thought of birds and stars and May; and if it so happened that your eyes turned to the gray piece that was Grandmother's, and the sky that was blue darkened and the rain fell, you had only to look at the pink piece that was Lizbeth's, or the blue and yellow that was Father's, to find the flowers and the sun again. Then the colors blended. Dandelions jingled, sleigh-bells and violets blossomed in the snow, and you slept—the sleep that makes little boys well.

The bees and the wind were humming in the cherry-trees, for it was May. You

Mother

were all alone, you and Mother, in the garden, where the white petals were falling, silently, like snow-flakes, and the birds were singing in the morning glow.

Your feet scampered down the paths. Your curls bobbed among the budding shrubs and vines. You leaped. You laughed. You sang. In your wide eyes blue of the great sky, green of the grasses. On your flushed cheeks sunshine and breeze. In your beating heart childhood and spring—a childhood too big, a spring too wonderful, for the smallness of one little, brimming boy.

"Look, Mother! See me jump."

"My!" she said.

"And see me almost stand on my head."

"Wonderful!"

"I know what I'll be when I grow to be a man, Mother."

"What will you be?"

In the Morning Glow

"A circus-rider."

"Gracious!" said she.

"On a big, white horse, Mother."

"Dear me!"

"And we'll jump 'way over the moon, Mother."

"The moon?"

"Yes, the moon. See!"

Then you jumped over the rake-handle. You were practising for the moon, you said.

"But maybe I *won't* be a circus-rider, Mother, after all."

"Maybe not," said she.

"Maybe I'll be President, like George Washington. Father said I could. Could I, Mother?"

"Yes—you might—some day."

"But the Jones boy couldn't, Mother."

"Why couldn't the Jones boy?"

"Because he swears and tells lies. I

Mother

don't. And George Washington didn't, Mother. I guess I won't be a circus-rider, after all."

"Oh, I'm glad of that, dear."

"No, I guess I'll keep right on, Mother — as long as I've started — and just be President."

"Oh, that will be fine," said she. She was sewing in the arbor, her lap filled with linen, her work-basket at her feet.

"Mother."

"Yes."

"I think I'd like to sing a song now."

Straight and proper you stood in the little path, your heels together, your hands at your side, and so you sang to her the song of the little duck:

"'Quack, quack,' said the Duck,
  'Quack, quack.'
  'Quack, quack,' said—"

You stopped.

In the Morning Glow

"Try it a little lower, dear."

"'Quack, quack,' said—"

"No, that's *too* low," you said. You tried again and started right that time and sang it through, the song of the little duck who

"'... wouldn't be a girl,
With only a curl,
I wouldn't be a girl, would you?'"

"Oh, it's beautiful," Mother said.

"Now it's your turn, Mother, to tell a story."

"A story?"

"Yes. About the violets."

"The violets?" she said, poising her needle, musingly. "The blue, blue violets—"

"As blue as the sky, Mother," you said, softly, for it is always in the hush of the garden that the stories grow.

Mother

"As blue as the sky," she said. "Ah, yes. Well, once there wasn't a violet in the whole world."

"Nor a single star," you said, awesomely, helping her. And as you sat there listening the world grew wider and wider—for when you are a little boy the world is always just as wide as your eyes.

"Not a violet or a single star in the whole world," Mother went on. "And what do you think? They just took little bits of the blue sky and sprinkled them all over the green world, and they were the first violets."

"And the stars, Mother?"

"Why, don't you see? The stars are the little holes they left in the blue sky, with the light of heaven shining through."

"Oh!" you said, softly. "Oh, Mother!"

And then, in the hush of the garden, you looked at her, and lo! her eyes were blue

In the Morning Glow

like the violets, and bright like the stars, for the light of heaven was shining through.

She was the most wonderful person in the whole world—who never did anything wrong, who knew everything, even who God was, watching, night and day, over little boys. Even the hairs of your head were numbered, she told you, and not a little bird died but He knew.

"And did He know when Cock Robin died, Mother?"

"Yes. He knew."

"And when I hurt my finger, Mother? Did He know then?"

"Yes, He knows everything."

"And was He sorry, Mother, when I hurt my finger?"

"Very sorry, dear."

"Then why did He *let* me hurt my finger—why?"

For a moment she did not speak.

Mother

"Dearie," she said at last, "I don't know. There are many things that nobody knows but God."

Hushed and wondering you sat in Mother's lap, for His eye was upon you. Somewhere up in the sky, above the clouds, you knew He was sitting, on a great, bright throne, with a gold crown upon His head and a sceptre in His hand—King of Kings and Lord of All. Down below Him on the green earth little birds were falling, little boys were hurting their fingers and crying in their Mothers' arms, and He saw them all, every one, little birds and little boys, but did not help them. You crept closer to Mother's bosom, flinging your arms about her neck.

"Don't let Him get me, Mother!"

"Why, darling, He loves you."

"Oh no, Mother—not like you do; not like you."

In the Morning Glow

The bees and the wind were in the apple-trees, for it was May. You were all alone, you and Mother, in the garden, where the white petals were falling, like snow-flakes, silently. In the swing Grandfather built for you, you sat swaying, to and fro, in the shadows; and the shadows swayed, to and fro, in the gale; and to and fro your thoughts swayed in your dreaming.

The wind sang in the apple-boughs, the flowering branches filled and bent, and all about you were the tossing, shimmering grasses, and all above you birds singing and flitting in the sky. And so you swayed, to and fro, till you were a sailor, in a blue suit, sailing the blue sea.

The wind sang in the rigging. The white sails filled and bent. Your ship scudded through the tossing, shimmering foam. Gulls screamed and circled in the

Mother

sky, . . . and so you sailed and sailed, with the sea-breeze in your curls . . .

The ship anchored.

The swing stopped.

You were only a little boy.

"Mother," you said, softly, for your voice was drowsy with your dream.

She did not hear you. She sat there in the arbor-seat, smiling at you, her hands idle, her sewing slipping from her knees. You did not know it then, but you do now —that to see the most beautiful woman in the whole world you must be her little boy.

There in her garden, in her lap, with her arms around you and her cheeks between your hands, you gazed, wondering, into the blue fondness of her eyes. You saw her lips, forever smiling at you, forever seeking your own. You heard her voice, sweet with love-words—

In the Morning Glow

"My dearest."

"Yes."

"My darling."

"Yes."

"My own dear little boy."

And then her arms crushing you to her breast; and then her lips; and then her voice again—

"Once in this very garden, in this very seat, Mother sat dreaming of you."

"Of me, Mother?"

"Of you. Here in the garden, with that very bush there red with blossoms, and the birds singing in these very trees. She dreamed that you were a little baby—a little baby, warm and soft in her arms—and while the wind sang to the flowers Mother sang you a lullaby, and you stretched out your hands to her and smiled; and then—ah, darling!"

"But it was a *dream*, Mother."

Mother

"It was only a dream—yes—but it came true. It came true on a night in June—the First of June, it was—"

"*My* birthday, Mother!"

"Your birthday, dear."

"Oh, Mother," you said, breathlessly—"what a beautiful dream!"

THE END

By ONOTO WATANNA

A JAPANESE NIGHTINGALE. A love story of Japan. Full-page Drawings in Color and unique Decorative Color Borders on every page, by the well-known Japanese artist GENJIRO YETO. Crown 8vo, Ornamented Cloth, Deckel Edges, Gilt Top (in a box), $2 00 *net*.

There could not easily be a more charming volume to look at than this, nor a more delightfully appealing romance to read.—*New York World.*

An idyl of the author's homeland, delicate in fancy and dainty in expression.—*Public Opinion.*

The author and the artist together have produced a charming work of art, as thoroughly imbued with the Japanese spirit as a bit of old Satsuma.—*Buffalo Express.*

"A Japanese Nightingale" is one of the daintiest and most exquisite of love stories; . . . indeed, so exquisite is her art, and so delightful the humor of her pages, that more than one critic has spoken of the story as "A Japanese Kentucky Cardinal."—*New York Journal.*

It is full of poetry and charm—*Current Literature.*

A delicious vein of humor runs through the story, especially in the love scenes, and the style is distinct with the lyrical delicacy of Japanese thought.—*Brooklyn Eagle.*

HARPER & BROTHERS, PUBLISHERS
NEW YORK AND LONDON

☞ *The above work will be sent by mail to any part of the United States, Canada, or Mexico, on receipt of the price. (Postage 15 cents.)*

By ONOTO WATANNA

THE WOOING OF WISTARIA. Frontispiece Portrait of Author. Post 8vo, Ornamented Cloth, $1 50.

This novel is a new departure in fiction. It is a strong, dramatic story of Japanese life by a Japanese author. The heroine, Wistaria, is a beautiful Japanese girl whose father, a soldier of rank, is cruelly wronged by a Prince of the reigning house. The daughter, swearing to avenge her father, falls in love with the son of the Prince without knowing his rank or position. From this dramatic motive the story is developed. It is not only a brilliant novel, but it has all the charm that made such a popular success of the author's first book, " A Japanese Nightingale."

HARPER & BROTHERS, Publishers
NEW YORK AND LONDON

☞ *The above work will be sent by mail, postage prepaid, to any part of the United States, Canada, or Mexico, on receipt of the price.*

By ANTHONY HOPE

THE INTRUSIONS OF PEGGY. Illustrated. Post 8vo, Ornamented Cloth, $1 50.

This is a novel with the interest of "Zenda" and the wit of the "Dolly Dialogues." It is a story of social and political life in London. A young widow goes to London to see life and make her way in the social world. She falls in with "Peggy," a most interesting character, pretty, attractive, ingenuous, and Bohemian. They meet with many adventures, most of which centre around a decidedly novel and interesting love interest. Peggy's "intrusions" into the happiness of herself and her friends is one of the motives of a novel as interesting in story as it is bright and unusual in dialogue.

HARPER & BROTHERS, PUBLISHERS
NEW YORK AND LONDON

☞ *The above work will be sent by mail, postage prepaid, to any part of the United States, Canada, or Mexico, on receipt of the price.*

By ROBERT W. CHAMBERS

THE MAID-AT-ARMS. Illustrated by Howard Chandler Christy. Post 8vo, Ornamented Cloth, $1 50.

Mr. Chambers has long since won a most enviable position among contemporary novelists. The great popular success of "Cardigan" makes this present novel of unusual interest to all readers of fiction. It is a stirring novel of American life in days just after the Revolution. It deals with the conspiracy of the great New York land-owners and the subjugation of New York Province to the British. It is a story with a fascinating love interest, and is alive with exciting incident and adventure. Some of the characters of "Cardigan" reappear in this new novel.

HARPER & BROTHERS, PUBLISHERS
NEW YORK AND LONDON

☞ *The above work will be sent by mail, postage prepaid, to any part of the United States, Canada, or Mexico, on receipt of the price.*

Trieste Publishing has a massive catalogue of classic book titles. Our aim is to provide readers with the highest quality reproductions of fiction and non-fiction literature that has stood the test of time. The many thousands of books in our collection have been sourced from libraries and private collections around the world.

The titles that Trieste Publishing has chosen to be part of the collection have been scanned to simulate the original. Our readers see the books the same way that their first readers did decades or a hundred or more years ago. Books from that period are often spoiled by imperfections that did not exist in the original. Imperfections could be in the form of blurred text, photographs, or missing pages. It is highly unlikely that this would occur with one of our books. Our extensive quality control ensures that the readers of Trieste Publishing's books will be delighted with their purchase. Our staff has thoroughly reviewed every page of all the books in the collection, repairing, or if necessary, rejecting titles that are not of the highest quality. This process ensures that the reader of one of Trieste Publishing's titles receives a volume that faithfully reproduces the original, and to the maximum degree possible, gives them the experience of owning the original work.

We pride ourselves on not only creating a pathway to an extensive reservoir of books of the finest quality, but also providing value to every one of our readers. Generally, Trieste books are purchased singly - on demand, however they may also be purchased in bulk. Readers interested in bulk purchases are invited to contact us directly to enquire about our tailored bulk rates. Email: customerservice@triestepublishing.com

You May Also Like

The Works of James Russell Lowell, Vol. VII. The Poetical Works of James Russell Lowell, in Four Volumes, Vol. I

James Russell Lowell

ISBN: 9780649640430
Paperback: 332 pages
Dimensions: 6.14 x 0.69 x 9.21 inches
Language: eng

Persecution and Tolerance: Being the Hulsean Lectures Preached Before the University of Cambridge in 1893-4

Mandell Creighton

ISBN: 9780649669356
Paperback: 164 pages
Dimensions: 6.14 x 0.35 x 9.21 inches
Language: eng

www.triestepublishing.com

You May Also Like

On Spermatorrhœa: Its Pathology, Results, and Complications

J. L. Milton

ISBN: 9780649663057
Paperback: 188 pages
Dimensions: 6.14 x 0.40 x 9.21 inches
Language: eng

Results of Astronomical Observations Made at the Sydney Observatory, New South Wales, in the Years 1877 and 1878

H. C. Russell

ISBN: 9780649692613
Paperback: 120 pages
Dimensions: 6.14 x 0.25 x 9.21 inches
Language: eng

www.triestepublishing.com

You May Also Like

1807-1907 The One Hundredth Anniversary of the incorporation of the Town of Arlington Massachusetts

Various

ISBN: 9780649420544
Paperback: 108 pages
Dimensions: 6.14 x 0.22 x 9.21 inches
Language: eng

Biennial report of the Board of State Harbor Commissioners, for the two fiscal years commencing July 1, 1890, and ending June 30, 1892

Various

ISBN: 9780649194292
Paperback: 44 pages
Dimensions: 6.14 x 0.09 x 9.21 inches
Language: eng

www.triestepublishing.com

You May Also Like

Biennial report of the Board of State Harbor Commissioners for the two fisca years. Commeneing July 1, 1884, and Ending June 30, 1886

Various

ISBN: 9780649199693
Paperback: 48 pages
Dimensions: 6.14 x 0.10 x 9.21 inches
Language: eng

Biennial report of the Board of state commissioners, for the two fiscal years, commencing July 1, 1890, and ending June 30, 1892

Various

ISBN: 9780649196395
Paperback: 44 pages
Dimensions: 6.14 x 0.09 x 9.21 inches
Language: eng

Find more of our titles on our website. We have a selection of thousands of titles that will interest you. Please visit

www.triestepublishing.com

Lightning Source UK Ltd.
Milton Keynes UK
UKOW01f1025231017
311488UK00009B/2563/P